THE PEOPLE'S
UNIVERSITY

'There is this difference between the youngest university in the empire and the oldest: Oxford was established by a king; the University of Queensland was established by the people.'

William Kidston, Premier of Queensland, 1909

THE PEOPLE'S UNIVERSITY

100 YEARS OF THE UNIVERSITY OF QUEENSLAND

Ben Robertson

First published 2010 by University of Queensland Press
PO Box 6042, St Lucia, Queensland 4067 Australia

www.uqp.com.au

Typeset in Arial Narrow 10.5/16pt by Post Pre-press Group, Brisbane
Printed in China by Everbest Printing Group

The University of Queensland Press uses papers that are natural, renewable and recyclable
products made from wood grown in sustainable forests. The logging and manufacturing
processes conform to the environmental regulations of the country of origin.

Cataloguing-in-Publication Data
National Library of Australia

Robertson, Ben
The people's university: 100 years of the University of Queensland

ISBN 9780702237683 (hbk)
      9780702238536 (pbk)
      9780702237935 (pdf)

University of Queensland – History.
Universities and colleges – Queensland – Brisbane – History.

378.9431

CONTENTS

The Eleanor Schonell Bridge provides pedestrian
access to the St Lucia campus from Dutton Park for
staff and students, as well as for members of the
community who come to the campus for relaxation.

PREFACE

'PEOPLE'S UNIVERSITY' IS A better description of the University of Queensland at the start of its second century than it was at its inception. As the years have rolled on, the institution now commonly known as 'UQ' has touched and enhanced the lives of an ever-expanding pool of people.

The modern UQ is more far-reaching and inclusive than even the most enlightened or imaginative of its initiators could have conceived. It would have been fanciful for the denizens of a city with a population of 137,000 to envisage a university of over 40,000 students. Even those who held that higher education should be open to rich and poor of both genders and all religions might not have dreamed that students would hail from more than 120 countries, that staff would collaborate with peers from all over the world, and that more than half of all students and staff would be women. It would have seemed improbable for an Aboriginal woman to be alumnus of the year, a UQ graduate to be the nation's first female governor-general and another UQ graduate to be Australia's first woman elected as a state premier.

Yet this is the reality of UQ, and its distance from the founders' imaginations cannot be glibly attributed to the changed and changing world. In fact the

University has had its own influence on the growth, prosperity, character and reputation of a Queensland that some now call 'the Smart State', and a nation with genuine aspirations of leadership in higher education, research and the commercialisation of innovation.

The UQ of today is the product of 'the people' – the staff, students, alumni, senators and supporters of its foundation century. Much of its contemporary strength is due to the strategies of past leaders. They attracted outstanding students and staff, expanded and diversified the fields of study, deepened the capacity in fundamental and applied research, developed a world's-best-practice commercialisation model, and created a physical environment that is as aesthetic as it is cutting-edge.

Crucially, these leaders also fostered long-term relationships with people and organisations throughout the world. Staff, students and alumni continue in the same vein, so that UQ now has a global network of friends and partners. Among much else, the network facilitates exchanges and internships, research and teaching collaborations, scholarships, and opportunities for high-end research. Our partnerships also enable people all over the planet to benefit from UQ innovation, and they free-up trade in the priceless currency of international and intercultural understanding.

The successes of late and living alumni and staff have established a pattern to be adopted and adapted for the future.

Internationalisation will go from strength to strength because this century will belong to graduates who can operate in diverse settings alongside friends, colleagues and clients from all over the world. Global themes will permeate all aspects of the University's activities. Increasingly, the experiences of students and the work of staff will impact on international developments as much as they are informed by them.

There is no question that UQ will stay the course as the people's institution. In a country as prosperous as Australia, every young person should be able realistically to reach for opportunities that will unlock their potential. UQ's role in optimising human potential will be limited only by the resolve of its people and the quality of partners who share the vision of a better world built on education and research.

It will always be called the University of Queensland, but UQ in its second century will be a people's university without borders.

Professor Paul Greenfield
Vice-Chancellor
University of Queensland

The walkway from the Great Court to the
Chancellors Place bus station

INTRODUCTION

Gum leaves and gumnuts, typical of the explicitly
Australian elements in the Great Court sculptures,
reflecting the popularity of the May Gibbs drawings
from the 1920s

IT'S HARD TO BELIEVE there was a time when the vast majority of
Queenslanders didn't want a university. Over a century ago few residents cared
about the intellectual yearnings of what some called the 'kid-gloved men' from
the elite grammar schools of Brisbane and the south-east corner. Far more
urgent was the need for more railways. One famous MLA from the agricultural
Darling Downs, William H Groom, labelled the idea of a university as another
worrying example of the 'Brisbanization' of the colony. A journalist from the
Courier wrote that universities were 'jolly places' that manufactured 'terribly
bumptious persons'. There were some brave men, including an archbishop,
who complained about the intellectual sterility of Queensland and the need for
a university to set higher academic standards. By all accounts their comments
didn't win them many supporters outside the capital, where more than three-
quarters of the population lived.

Despite these early setbacks, and while swimming against the tide of
public opinion, plans for a university slowly gained traction. For nearly forty
years, from 1870 to 1909, the positives and negatives of the idea were argued
in parliament and thrashed out in the public domain led by the determined
University Extension Movement, which coincidentally was launched in
1893 with the help of William Groom's son, Littleton E Groom, who was
its secretary. Discussions at Groom family functions about the need for a
university must have been quite animated. Finally, in December 1909, the
University of Queensland Act was signed. The names of the members of the
first senate (the twenty men who were to govern the university) appeared
in the *Queensland Government Gazette* on 16 April 1910 along with the
implementation of the previous year's Bill, and this has become the date
that marks official celebrations. The University of Queensland was now in
existence.

In the end the government decided to move in 1909 because there was a good public relations spin: it had been fifty years since Queensland had separated from New South Wales and become a colony in its own right and what better way to celebrate its Golden Jubilee than to start a university. The main condition stipulated by the government, though, was that it be a 'people's university', distinct from any other in Australia and free from the sterile thinking of the past. In keeping with this theme of change, the incoming governor of Queensland, Sir William MacGregor, was to be relocated from Government House at George Street in the City to make way for the first site. He was told of the change of address as he was leaving England and was none too pleased. To help ease the pain, MacGregor, a no-nonsense Scotsman from Aberdeen trained in medicine and later an experienced colonial administrator, was appointed the first chancellor of the new university. Known for his velvet sledgehammer approach to problem solving, he and the senate set about the task of creating a world-class institution that Queensland could be proud of. None of the men involved had any experience of running a university.

It would be almost a year before the first professors (informally known as the 'Big Four') took their places at the University of Queensland. The advertised annual salary was a princely £900 and the government scoured both Australia and Great Britain to find them, even securing the services of what these days would be called a head-hunter, based in London. The selection process was quite rigorous: as well as being intelligent, the candidates had to possess robust health and a pioneering spirit. Such were the requirements for academic life in a tough frontier society like Queensland.

Classes started on 14 March 1911. There were eighty-three students, including twenty-three women. In his first mathematics lecture Professor Henry

UQ's first chancellor, Sir William MacGregor, at Old Government House

Sir Llew Edwards Building, which houses modern
teaching facilities and sets the standard for university
learning space design, 2009

Priestley, an Englishman described as coming from an illustrious lineage, found himself without chalk for the blackboard. A century later and the University of Queensland has more than 40,000 students from 129 countries. Next-Generation Learning Spaces using touch-screen computers and wireless technology have eliminated the need for chalk.

The University's relocation from Old Government House to the expansive grounds of the St Lucia site of today was not without its problems. St Lucia, it was argued, was too far away from the general population to be a people's

The cloister of the Great Court features university coats of arms from around the world.

Mary Emelia Mayne, c. 1890

Dr James Mayne, c. 1890

Law lecturer Quentin Bryce in 1978. After a number of senior jobs and a five-year term as governor of Queensland, Quentin Bryce became the first female governor-general of Australia in 2008.

university. The land was also prohibitively expensive. The move became possible only after Dr James O'Neil Mayne and his sister Mary Emelia Mayne donated over £50,000 in 1927 so the Brisbane City Council could resume the 274 acres of sugar cane, arrowroot and pineapple farming land at St Lucia for the University. An alternative site also under consideration was on the hilly slopes of Victoria Park near the General Hospital (now the Royal Brisbane and Women's Hospital), which was much closer to the central business district and public transport. A narrow vote in the university senate decided the issue, and even then it was nearly overturned as the Great Depression and a lack of finance delayed St Lucia's development. When the impressive Main Building (later renamed the Forgan Smith Building in honour of the premier who made the money available) was finally constructed in 1939 it looked strangely out of place standing high on a hill overlooking the vast rural landscape. General Sir Thomas Blamey commandeered the building during World War II, establishing the headquarters of the Allied Land Forces there as the battle for control of the Pacific raged close to home. The first students described the new site as a barren and inhospitable place. Some academic departments had to make do with old huts and decrepit farm buildings.

After the war there was confusion and anger directed at the senate, especially from the student body, because of the constant delays in moving from George Street to St Lucia. While it may have seemed to take an eternity, over thirty years in fact, in the end few people could have imagined how the area would be transformed, now dotted with lakes, parks, sporting grounds, residential colleges, sculptures and over 150 buildings representing differing architectural styles. At the University's centre is the heritage-listed Great Court surrounded by the noble sandstone edifices of the pre- and post-war years, the modern University Art Museum that has breathed new life into Mayne

Hall by cleverly using natural light, and the V-shaped Sir Llew
Edwards Building with its cutting-edge teaching facilities and
environmental features of water harvesting, solar panels and
strategic shading.

Towards the end of the last century, the University
consolidated with the Queensland Agricultural College at
Gatton, while a new campus was added in Ipswich, catering
for the needs of students living along the growth corridor west
of Brisbane. The new Eleanor Schonell Bridge from the St
Lucia campus across the river to Dutton Park in the southern
suburbs has gone some way towards alleviating the traffic and
parking problems of the past. Dedicated for bus, pedestrian
and cyclist access only, the bridge was a long time coming. The
Brisbane City Council and the state government promised to
deliver a bridge before the University first moved to St Lucia,
but numerous budget overruns meant that the project was
continually delayed, before being quietly shelved and finally
forgotten. A first estimate for a suspension bridge costing nearly
£200,000 gave everyone a shock from which it took over eighty years to
recover.

UQ's first Nobel laureate, Professor Peter Doherty

The achievements of the University of Queensland as a place of learning
are formidable. The University is among the top eight 'sandstone' institutions
in the country (known as the Group of Eight, the equivalent of America's Ivy
League) and is ranked among the top fifty universities and colleges in the
world. From its alumni, it has a Nobel laureate, an Oscar winner, state premiers,
governors and governors-general, High Court justices, Olympic medallists and
celebrated novelists. In 2006 Professor Ian Frazer was named Australian of

Geoffrey Rush (top) in the production *Bacchoi* at the Schonell Theatre in 1970. Rush went on to a celebrated cinematic career, winning an Academy Award for his role in the movie *Shine* in 1997.

the Year for his work on a vaccine for cervical cancer that will save hundreds of thousands of lives here and overseas. Professor Frazer first made the discovery with the late Dr Jian Zhou nearly twenty years ago while working at the University of Queensland. Professor Frazer now heads the Diamantina Institute for Cancer, Immunology and Metabolic Medicine, which is one of seven research institutes of the University of Queensland. Hundreds of millions of dollars have been invested in areas like bioscience, so more groundbreaking discoveries can be expected in the future. It is worth remembering that when classes first began at the University there was only one laboratory and it had no sink, so students used buckets for their experiments.

Over the past one hundred years the university senate has at times strayed from the state government's promise to create a people's university, but it has

The bridge over the lake is part of a walkway connecting the engineering precinct with the University Lakes bus stop.

never completely lost touch with it. The University operates from fifty sites throughout Queensland – from hospitals to islands in the Great Barrier Reef, and it even has a long lease over an experimental mine, conveniently located nearby at suburban Indooroopilly in Brisbane's western suburbs. Students from throughout the state can board at the numerous colleges based on the St Lucia campus (as well as the Halls of Residence at Gatton), and the public is encouraged to enjoy the walking and jogging tracks, cafés, parks, libraries and museums. Picnicking around the lakes off College Road at St Lucia, feeding the ducks and afterwards taking a stroll through the jacarandas, whose brilliant purple flowers signal the start of preparations for final exams, is something that many local residents have done at some stage in their lives. From modest beginnings, the University now has 150 student clubs and societies including thirty-three sports clubs. A three-level gymnasium and multi-purpose indoor sports centre, a synthetic athletics track, an Olympic-size swimming pool and twenty-one floodlit tennis courts are some of the world-class facilities that are available for all Queenslanders and visitors to enjoy.

The centenary of the University of Queensland is a milestone that would make its academic pioneers proud. One hundred years on and it is still the people's university.

Bougainvilleas in bloom, St Lucia campus

Jacarandas and sandstone, two recognisable
University of Queensland features

CHAPTER 1

THE
EARLY
YEARS

UQ's first four professors, (from left) Professor Michie, Professor Gibson, Professor Priestley and Professor Steele. Gibson served for a short period only and did not later have a building named after him.

SETTING UP A NEW university wasn't all serious business. Most of the lecturers were quite young and delighted in mixing with the students at numerous social gatherings. Due to their youthfulness, the staff were sometimes mistaken for students themselves. There are reports of Henry C Richards, the University's first professor of geology, pirouetting around the dance floor in his tie and tails at a function while munching on a hot meat pie. He had gained earlier notoriety during a cricket match between staff and students when he landed on a fresh cow pat while attempting a catch and much to the delight of the crowd auctioned off his shirt to the highest bidder. Richards went on to become a mighty figure at the University and had a building named after him in 1951.

Professor of Classics was 29-year-old Scotsman John Lundie Michie, coincidentally from the same corner of the world as Chancellor MacGregor, which is perhaps why he was chosen over another candidate who was considered by the overseas talent scouts to be better qualified. Michie had been an academic success at Cambridge and was a superb athlete, but he had little teaching experience. Despite the controversy, he proved to be an excellent choice and was much loved by the staff and students. Known for his wisdom and shyness, he devoted the rest of his life to ensuring that the University of Queensland was a success. Professor Henry Priestley managed to overcome the lack of chalk in his first mathematics lecture and was also well liked by the students and his colleagues. He was remembered for his caring attitude, especially towards concerned parents, and was coach of the women's hockey team. Like Michie, he also spent the rest of his life at the University of Queensland. London-born Alexander Gibson, a professional engineer but without a degree, was chosen from the ranks of the Australian-based applicants as the senate was seeking someone with an intimate knowledge of the country's manufacturing and construction industries. Gibson's stay as head of Engineering was relatively short due to his service as a reserve officer overseas during World War I and his subsequent resignation from the University in January 1919, but he designed and built the engineering laboratories that were applauded as being the best in Australia at the time. Bertram Dillon Steele, who lodged his application in Brisbane, was the oldest professor by quite a few years, at forty, and had a wealth of teaching experience, having taught at universities in Great Britain, Canada and Australia. Described as a brilliant lecturer who was always immaculately groomed, he became the first president of the Board of Faculties and was pivotal in providing advice to the senate on how a university should be run. He was the University's first 'professor emeritus', a title bestowed on him when he resigned the Chair of Chemistry in December 1930 after twenty years' loyal service. His wife was well known for the quality of her scones, which she baked for third-year chemistry students.

From day one staff expressed their frustration at the unsuitability of the rooms at Government House and the equipment they'd been given to run their courses. Professors Priestley and Michie landed in Brisbane from Great Britain only four weeks before classes began. Priestley later wrote: 'We are housed in a building inadequate in size and unsuitable in design. It is riddled with white ants; leaking roofs and frequent and falling ceilings are not unknown.' A team of seven lecturers, five assistant lecturers, one evening lecturer and one demonstrator in chemistry helped the Big Four, arriving in dribs and drabs as the first academic year progressed. In Biology, lecturer Dr Thomas Johnston finally made an appearance in term three. As he hastily tried to catch up, the government seconded him to help eradicate a prickly pear epidemic, thus causing even more confusion. Classes had already started before the first registrar, the impressively named FWS Cumbrae Stewart, sent the government an outline of

Old Government House, George Street, which was a UQ site from 1910 to 1972

what the departments needed in terms of equipment – £16,000 for Engineering, £3,000 for Physics, £2,500 for Chemistry, £1,000 for the Arts faculty, £700 for Geology and £600 for Biology – thus establishing a hierarchy that would endure for years to come. There was also an immediate need for £17,400, he wrote, for the departments as a group to begin operating.

The early academic plan was to establish faculties of Arts, Science and Engineering and to create chairs in Classics, Mathematics, Chemistry and

Women undergraduates at the Exhibition Hall, 1911. With mortar boards on their heads, they had to carry their sun hats.

Engineering. To bring lawyers and doctors who had graduated elsewhere into the fold meant the temporary creation of faculties of Law and Medicine so the university could grant honorary degrees. These honorary graduates would eventually form the first University Council. The pattern of the first academic year was three terms of ten weeks' duration each. The Bachelor of Arts and Bachelor of Science degrees were three years long, and the students would study three subjects in each year. Engineering was to take four years along similar lines. The administration team attempting to ensure that things ran smoothly at the new university was overworked, underfunded and understaffed. The team was referred to in some reports as the 'happy family'. Whether this was a sarcastic reference or the honest truth is not known. In 1925 there were nine positions besides those of the registrar, who was paid a handsome £500 per annum. Assisting him were two staff on loan from the Department of Public Instruction, one of whom was typist Olga de Tuetey who was paid £52 a year. Administration staff were expected to be multi-skilled, well-behaved and devoted to their jobs. In the early years one man was sacked for drink driving (motor cars were still a rarity in Brisbane, so it must have caused quite a stir), and another was severely reprimanded for playing sport on the weekend and breaking his arm. University janitor Walter Wyche was obviously a humorous character and a favourite of the students, described in an annual report as 'an institution in his own right'. He was often referred to in songs at degree ceremonies.

At the original Government House site there were no student common rooms, although the women had a cloakroom that opened onto a courtyard where they could eat their lunch and drink cups of tea. In June 1912 the senate

Wordsmith's Café, a popular meeting place situated next to the University of Queensland Press. UQP first published Peter Carey's *Oscar and Lucinda* and *True History of the Kelly Gang*, both of which won the Booker Prize.

University of Queensland staff in 1922. To the original professors have been added Professors Hawken, Mayo, Richards and Parnell.

Roger Hawken, Professor of Engineering, c. 1920, and later a founder of the Institution of Engineers, Australia

resolved to provide separate common rooms and a reading room for both sexes. The men's common room was a busy and noisy space where they sometimes practised for Commemoration ceremonies. Preparations for the Commemoration procession would begin the week before, when wagons were driven onto the university grounds and students worked around the clock putting up their banners and decorations. They made fun of the politics of the day, although the senate preferred them to aim their barbs at the Commonwealth rather than the state, so as not to place at risk the University's £10,000 annual endowment. From the start, the students took great delight in rebelling against everything the senate ordered them not to do. The public had a free show as the procession wound its way down the city streets, with procession floats bombarded by water bombs and paper missiles thrown by public servants from the Queensland Government Printing Office and the Taxation Department. A conga line of students went into city stores and even onto trams and was tolerated by a bemused public, at least in the early days. By 1932 things were starting to get out of hand and the students were criticised for being 'Varsity Yahoos'. In 1937 the police paid a 'courtesy call' to inspect the procession floats and some were banned. This had a deadening effect on festivities and the following year the procession was described as being 'short and dismal'. Undeterred, the students focused more on disrupting the degree ceremony held in the recently completed City Hall in Adelaide Street. Previously the ceremony had been held in the Exhibition Hall on Gregory Terrace.

Commemoration was the highlight of the social year. Women attending the Commemoration Ball had to have special permission from their residences or colleges, and had to clearly state their intended whereabouts before and after the ball and who would be accompanying them. This requirement was not open for debate and survived for more than half a century at Women's College. Cabs were still drawn by horses and were expensive, so for most students long walks were the order of the day. Most resided in the colleges at Kangaroo Point, a suburb located across the river from the University. The students used rowing boats by day or the Edward Street steam ferry that closed just before midnight. From 1912 the colleges contributed substantially to the social scene. Before their arrival, the senate was forced to publish a list of approved boarding houses, as most of the public houses were deemed unsuitable and unsafe. In March 1912 the Presbyterians established Emmanuel College on Wickham Terrace. St John's was set up by the Anglican Church on River Terrace at Kangaroo Point and was soon joined nearby by the Methodist-run King's College. In March 1914 the non-denominational Women's College also set up operations at Kangaroo Point on Shafston

The Sir James Foots Building, at the bottom of Staff House Road, houses the Sustainable Minerals Institute.

Dorothy Hill, the first female professor at an Australian university, 1930

Long-serving senate member and supporter of UQ, the Most Reverend James Duhig, c. 1915

Avenue. Four years later St Leo's was founded for Catholic men, and its sister college, Duchesne, was started in 1937. The concentration of St John's, King's and Women's College at Kangaroo Point made that area an early focus for picnics and boat trips up the river.

As befitting a state obsessed by sport, much of the early social life of the University revolved around athletic pursuits. Formed in June 1911, the Sports Union was the first undergraduate association and it began with almost a hundred members. Inter-collegiate rowing, cricket and football were immediately popular, and inter-varsity contests began in 1913. The Sports Union had trouble finding grounds for the many games; this was especially the case for cricket, because the Brisbane City Council would not let the Sports Union prepare practice wickets on the Government House domain. Tennis also posed a problem. There were superb courts but they were soon set aside for the exclusive use of staff, who weren't about to give them up for the students. Other social groups quickly followed the Sports Union, including the Student Christian Movement, which sought senate approval to meet on university grounds, and the Musical Society, the Women's Club, the Debating Society and the Dramatic Club.

There were two political issues that stood in the way of the University becoming a people's university. The hope of free tuition was abandoned early on when the exorbitant costs of running a university were realised. This caused uproar, but by far the most debated issue of the early years was matriculation. The first students were admitted to the University on temporary and rather lenient matriculation arrangements. Almost immediately there was a little head scratching about the suitability of some people who'd been let into the University. One student in the early years was reprimanded for being drunk and singing songs on a geology field trip and was suspended and fined £5 by the Board of Faculties. On the subject of matriculation, insults were hurled under parliamentary privilege and heated articles appeared in the press. Some people, including a future chancellor, argued that the state school inspectors should decide access to the University, because a people's university needed to be accessible to people from all classes. The government wanted a streamlined state education system right through to tertiary level, and it was against studies such as the 'dead languages' that provided no help in the struggle of modern life. The only subjects in favour with the government were engineering and chemistry. The senate under the chairmanship of MacGregor held the opposite view and made it clear that it would not be subservient to the government, even though it was the government that provided most of the funding. MacGregor proclaimed the need for high, internationally accepted matriculation standards to ensure the standing of its graduates. 'There must be no backdoor in Australia to easy degrees!' he said, nor could he understand why scientists and engineers thought themselves above the need to study languages. The *Courier* applauded the desire for high standards, while others lamented the possible creation of a 'shabby copy of Oxford'. The newspaper asked whether Darwin, Huxley or Edison would have qualified for admission to the University of Queensland and worried that some academics seemed hell-bent on making the institution a bastion of exclusivity. In the end the senate got its way and sent the University on a clear path of decision-making free from government influence and control.

The matriculation arrangements for those who enrolled in 1911 ensured that most undergraduates came from the grammar schools, although there were also a lot of older students who had come through University Extension

Dorothy Hill pushing a float as the Commemoration Week procession leaves Old Government House, then part of the University, 1920s.

Women's College student residents and the principal, Miss Freda Bage,1922

courses that had been available since 1893. These older men and women are believed to have had a steadying influence within the undergraduate body, except maybe at Commemoration time in April when everyone went a little crazy. The influence of ex-soldiers in 1919 also contributed to the maturity of the student body. Some students benefited from the twenty government scholarships available annually. Tuition was paid for three years and included a £26 maintenance allowance for those who came from places outside Brisbane. Vice-Chancellor Reginald Roe, a former headmaster at Brisbane Grammar, believed that the number of scholarships in Queensland was more generous than anywhere else in Australia. He enthused that this generosity would throw open the door of the University to Queensland's poorer classes. When John Douglas Story, the government's main representative on the first senate and a future vice-chancellor, appeared at a prize-giving ceremony on the central coast in 1913, he stressed that the University of Queensland was not a place for Brisbane's elite or the well-off from other towns with grammar schools. Rather, it was open to all students who finished Senior. By 1917 some politicians were sceptical of this claim, as fees, which the Labor members had opposed as a barrier to popular participation, were slowly being built into the system. The University was always short of money and with fees it was more and more reliant on the ranks of the wealthy at the expense of the battlers. The *Darling Downs Advocate* ridiculed the senate for being less willing than universities down south to open its doors to the intelligent children of poor people. For the time being, the University ignored its critics and still demanded Latin or Greek for its arts students and a modern language for the engineers and scientists.

By the inauguration ceremony of June 1911, where honorary degrees were awarded to doctors, lawyers and other professional people around Brisbane as a gesture of goodwill, it was written that spirits were a 'little too much inclined towards rowdyism'. Degree ceremonies became noisy affairs, with the first undergraduates poking fun at the establishment by rewording the verses to popular songs, much to the horror of the dignitaries present. By 1914, when

Enjoying the spring sunshine at the St Lucia campus

the first home-bred students were graduating, the situation had deteriorated further. The students defied the orders of the police commissioner and had a merry procession through the city streets while engaging in what was reported as 'fanciful pranks'. There was considerable evidence that the consumption of alcohol helped lower inhibitions. Chancellor MacGregor gave a long-winded speech that year. It started after lunch and was still going strong well into the evening. As there was no electricity, guests struck matches brought in from the Belle Vue Hotel to view proceedings. After World War I the University's first big Commemoration procession featured carts decorated with streamers and banners, and at the degree ceremony afterwards students threw 'Tom Thumb' firecrackers at the premier and eggs into the crowd. A fire panic that started at His Majesty's Theatre, where students sometimes practised for Commemoration, was blamed on the young men from the University who, as one journalist wrote, were expressing their idea of humour. When chickens and ducks were released into the crowd during a degree ceremony in the 1930s there was widespread debate about whether taxpayer contributions to the University were being used wisely.

The avenue of Canary Island date palm trees at the heart of the Gatton campus

University women's hockey team, 1918

In the early years the senate believed that its responsibility to students was not purely academic. The university had a social and moral responsibility to consider as well. Chancellor MacGregor was concerned that some students had to pass public houses on their way to and from the University. He insisted that women and men should sit apart at degree ceremonies. A young lady from the Women's College was instructed to put her hair up while on campus and

John (Jack) Fryer, c. 1915

UQ Inter-varsity Hockey Team, 1930

some students complained about being reprimanded on the ferry by staff for the untidiness of their outfits. The *Queensland University Magazine* editor was nearly sacked for publishing a satirical article that made fun of the administration and academic staff. The students held their ground, complaining that the discipline at university should not be the same as at school. They would not tolerate being treated like naughty schoolchildren. In the second term of 1911 the students had had enough of the overly paternalistic authority and decided they needed their own voice. A conference of delegates from day and evening students established a University of Queensland Union (later to become known commonly as the Student Union), which duly sought senate recognition. It was a long time coming and involved application after rejected application. In 1921 the University of Queensland Union was officially accepted by the senate and assumed responsibility for the political and social aspects of student life on campus. Fast-forward ninety years and the Student Union now represents the interests of over 40,000 students across five campuses, and owns and operates several businesses, including a cinema, a second-hand bookshop, a pizza café and a bar.

Students were discouraged from making their opinions known on political subjects, but when war was declared in 1914 this rule was substantially relaxed. The senate was keen to throw its weight behind the war effort and made it known that students who enlisted would not suffer any loss of credit for study already done. Among many, Professor Gibson and registrar Cumbrae Stewart were released on full pay for military work on the condition that they paid back the extra money they earned. In 1915 the University established a War Committee to assist defence authorities during the munitions crisis, and eight chemists from the University were sent to England to work. Despite a depleted staff and student

Brickwork and sandstone columns under way for the Main Building, later called the Forgan Smith Building after the premier of the day, in 1938

body, it was business as usual. During the hostilities, thirty-three University staff and students were killed in action or died later from their wounds. One who did return was John Denis (Jack) Fryer, but he passed away in 1923 from injuries he received in France after being gassed in the trenches. His life was commemorated in the Fryer Library that was set up using a donation of £10 from his friends in the Dramatic Society. English lecturer Dr Frederick Robinson (fondly known as Doc Robbie) also helped out and generously donated volumes of Australian literature from his private collection. Entry to the library was through Doc Robbie's study. The Fryer Library at St Lucia now houses a

The first of the Great Court buildings under construction in 1947. Their proximity to the river is much more obvious than it is today.

collection of Australian literature, including rare books and manuscripts, with very few rivals in the world. When the Great War ended in 1918, students wanted to study subjects like engineering and chemistry, believing that that was where the jobs would be in the future, but from 1923 the commerce and arts subjects, previously thought of as inferior, became more popular. By 1936 there were 357 day students, 389 evening students and 403 external students, of whom more than half were studying Arts and Law. There were 109 in Commerce, 118 in Science, 41 in Engineering and 17 in Agriculture. In the new professional faculties, 74 were enrolled in Medicine, 40 in Dentistry, and only 4 in Veterinary Science.

From its inception, the people's university served the whole of the state. From 1912, a department of Correspondence Studies, founded by Thomas E Jones and later called External Studies, made it possible for students in the far-flung reaches of Queensland to study for a degree from home. By the 1940s, there was a special library (later named the Thatcher Memorial Library for Thomas Thatcher, Director of External Studies from 1938) to dispatch books to external students, vacation schools were conducted in Brisbane and, in the 1950s under director Edward Ringrose, a team of young lecturers travelled around the state, conducting tutorials with student groups in provincial towns. Across the state, teachers in particular, but also bank clerks, aspiring lawyers, many women who had earlier missed opportunities for a higher education and others worked towards their degrees. The external studies program was a stand-out leader in Australia for many years, ending in the late 1980s as other universities took up involvement in distance education.

Despite all the excitement surrounding the establishment of the new university, by 1912 it was abundantly clear to everyone using the facilities that Government House would never become a permanent home. Termites were destroying the library and in some lectures students were taking notes while standing outside and peering in through the windows. Premier Digby Denham was bombarded with requests for help. Land at Yeronga Park was offered and then withdrawn. Victoria Park was considered the most suitable site, although the cost of the buildings and to move equipment made the venture seem an impossibility. A site near the one now occupied by the Medical School at Herston was secured by statute in case the situation changed in the future. It was at about this time that a pocket of land in the remote farmland of St Lucia was first looked at by the senate. The farming land would have to be resumed and would cost a large sum, which nobody was willing to put up, but there was enough room for university buildings, acres of parkland and perhaps even a teaching hospital. Some senate members claimed it would be the envy of every university in Australia. Premier Denham quickly put an end to all this ridiculous

St Lucia campus in 2006, with the GPN4 building under construction. It was later named the Sir Llew Edwards Building in honour of the long-serving chancellor.

The Queensland Brain Institute Building, completed in 2007, has a striking four-storey atrium space, which features a unique piece of art created by the well-known Australian artist Fiona Hall. The work is incorporated via an interlayer into the full-height, glass laboratory walls.

dreaming. He assured the senate that Government House would be sufficient for their needs for another fifty years.

With the departure of Chancellor MacGregor to Great Britain on his retirement, Sir Pope Cooper, the Chief Justice of Queensland, took over as chancellor in April 1915. During its first term the senate had dealt with just about every aspect of university life and some members found handing over the reins of power difficult. The matters that senate members argued over were quite trivial, including on one occasion the use of a lawn-mower. Professors Gibson, Michie and Priestley joined the second senate in 1916. JD Story remained a member, but Vice-Chancellor Roe, who had been there from the beginning, was dropped, as was John Laskey Woolcock, the elder statesman of the University Extension Movement. In the end there were only four survivors from the first senate, and for many years there was a great deal of bitterness towards the state government about the way things had been handled. In 1923 the first woman, Freda Bage, was elected to the senate. She was the head of Women's College and was also the first departmental head of Biology. That same year also saw a graduate of the University, Edwin J Stanley, being elected to the senate for the first time.

The chancellor at the University of Queensland in the early years was never a mere figurehead. The vice-chancellor's position wasn't comparable to today's role either; back then his main duty was that of deputy chairman of the senate. It is unthinkable in modern times that a university vice-chancellor could hold the position while still working in another job, but Dr William N Robertson managed this while still in medical practice. The situation changed in 1938 when JD Story replaced him as vice-chancellor. Story retired from the public service the following year and was able to become the first full-time vice-chancellor (amazingly, he wasn't paid for his services, regarding the job as a labour of love), thus helping to bring the University nearer to the Australian standard, where the vice-chancellor is effectively the university's CEO. It wouldn't be until his successor, Professor Fred Schonell, took over in 1960, though, that the state government would provide funding to pay the vice-chancellor.

Like most institutions and businesses around the world, the University of Queensland was stretched to the very end of its financial reserves when funds dried up overnight following the Wall Street Crash in 1929. The turning point for the University came in 1935, when the state government led by Premier William Forgan Smith gave generously in all directions, even promising to restore staff salaries, which had been in serious decline. Student numbers actually rose through the Depression years, so that by 1936 when the University was emerging from its troubles there were over 1,000 students. At the Silver Jubilee celebrations of 1935 the senate awarded an honorary doctorate to Premier Forgan Smith. (Premier William Kidston had been awarded one twenty-five years earlier when the University was established.) An Open Day, billed as 'Gown meets Town', was organised and professors decked out in all their academic finery performed experiments in labs and workshops for the public. Red carpets were borrowed from Parliament House and a marquee was erected on the tennis courts for supper as a regimental band and then fireworks entertained the guests.

Compared with the other states, the number of people willing to donate to the University of Queensland in the early years was a cause for great concern. Financial benefactors founded the University of Adelaide. From the start the University of Sydney had bequests that financed seven chairs and ten

Corellas are now regular and noisy visitors to the St Lucia campus

Until the move to St Lucia, the University expanded its presence in George St. The Engineering Building was still in use in 1959 when this photo was taken.

lectureships, while the University of Melbourne had gifts of over £300,000 – the equivalent of twenty years of government assistance. Student publications criticised the senate for not showing enough initiative in raising money from the private sector, while the *Courier* lampooned those businessmen who made their money in Queensland but didn't give to the University.

However, the University did have some private funding in the early years. In 1915 it received the generous Walter and Eliza Hall benefaction, which helped create three fellowships as well as being a source of income for future years. Another major benefaction of the early years occurred in 1919 from wealthy Riverina grazier Samuel McCaughey. The McCaughey bequest gave the University an annual income of £7,500, about three-quarters of the state government's original annual endowment. The John Darnell bequest of 1931 allowed for a chair in English and also included £5,000 for the university library, and the James Forsyth gift of £10,000 went towards the cost of a permanent library building. The government must have been impressed or embarrassed, because it agreed to contribute the remainder of the money needed for the new library to be completed. The foundation stone for the library building was laid in 1935, in celebration of the University's Silver Jubilee. The building is now the administrative headquarters of the Queensland University of Technology.

Clair House, one of the heritage buildings on the Ipswich campus, was originally designed as accommodation for patients at the then Ipswich Hospital for the Insane.

Towards the end of 1932 the University was offered the gift of the Masonic Hall in Alice Street, which was to provide a home for dentists, anatomy students and engineers in the years to come, relieving the overcrowding in George Street. A £20,000 bequest by William Robertson in 1933 helped fund a chair in Agriculture, and the founding of a full Law Faculty was made possible by a £20,000 endowment from businessman Thomas C Beirne, also to celebrate the Silver Jubilee. Earlier a gift of £10,000 by Kate Garrick and her mother, Dame Catherine Garrick, in memory of Sir James Garrick helped create the Garrick Chair of Law; this outraged the Queensland branch of the British Medical Association, which wanted the money for a medical school.

As generous as these early bequests were, by far the most influential donation in the early years came from the Mayne family. In 1923 Dr James Mayne and his sister gave a property gift of 693 acres at the junction of Moggill Creek and the Brisbane River, which became the University's Moggill Farm and later the Veterinary Science Farm at Pinjarra Hills. Philanthropy must have sat well with the Mayne family, because four years later they gave £50,000 (and later another £10,000) to the Brisbane City Council so the farming land at St Lucia that the senate had been interested in many years earlier could be acquired for the University. Without the Mayne bequest, the University would today probably be located at Victoria Park between Spring Hill and Herston. This, of course, would have set it on a very different path in terms of its development.

In 2006 the Biological Sciences Refectory under the Biological Sciences Library was replaced by Darwin's Café, an indoor/outdoor eating area shaded by palms, which can be accessed from the ground floor of the library.

The first two decades of the University of Queensland were about establishing a 'people's university'. The next two decades were about expanding the vision. A Faculty of Commerce was established in December 1925 and a Faculty of Agriculture a few years later. But the greatest academic leap forward was in the establishment of Law and Dentistry faculties in 1935, and Medicine and Veterinary Science faculties in 1936, which coincidentally was the same year that the government announced the construction of the new buildings at St Lucia. It was expected that the buildings would cost £300,000 and the equipment another £200,000 – a huge miscalculation as it turned out, because that amount also included plans for a three-span steel bridge of the largest kind in Australia. Of course, no one on the senate knew how quickly costs would increase or that another world war was just around the corner. Premier Forgan Smith laid the first foundation stone for the Main Building on 6 March 1937, although the stone had to be moved to the tower after a shift in alignment forced a change in the plans when construction started a year later. Despite a brief strike by workers over the use of cheap labour, progress went ahead quickly and by the end of 1938 was on schedule. The Main Building was finished in 1939, and praise was heaped on the structure, described by some visitors as 'the finest building to be seen anywhere', although due to the start of World War II there would be a long period before the University had the opportunity to use it for teaching purposes. (It was renamed the Forgan Smith Building in 1967.) By this time, though, it was realised that £500,000 was not nearly enough to include all the intended plans. The government had also promised loans to the colleges to enable them to move to St Lucia. Again, the estimate of £40,000 each was manifestly inadequate. As the senate looked at ways to cut costs, work at St Lucia was confined to the library, and the chemistry and geology buildings. A report about St Lucia in

The Australian Army under General Blamey took over the new buildings at the St Lucia campus during World War II, while the students remained at the George Street campus in the city.

The UQ Centre, completed in 2002 beside Oval Number 4, is the current St Lucia graduations venue. It is in close proximity to major sporting facilities and is also used for netball, volleyball and basketball games.

Semper Floreat in September 1940 read: 'It is growing slowly and laboriously as a great tree stretches itself up from the blank earth and adds over the years the imperceptible inch upon inch to girth and height.'

In July 1942 the senate learned that the Australian military would be moving into the buildings at St Lucia, and the books, documents and museum pieces already transferred there should be returned to Government House. Veterinary Science was one of the first casualties of the war, losing its building at Yeerongpilly to the American Army in 1942. In February 1943 soldiers even took over the Masonic Hall in Alice Street, displacing Anatomy and Engineering, although Professor Roger Hawken from Engineering was allowed to keep one room after making his displeasure felt. The University became more integrated in the war effort than it had been in the Great War of 1914–18. Special courses on first aid, cooking, demolition and physical education were held on campus. Of these, physical education went on to become part of the curriculum, which didn't sit well with the traditionalists. Trenches were dug around Old Government House and air-raid shelters were constructed, while temporary buildings of every shape and size were erected wherever a vacant piece of ground could be found. By now, building materials were in short supply and despite pleas from the senate for more money the state government cut off funds. The war was on Australia's doorstep and building work was officially suspended. The transfer to St Lucia was postponed until the war was over.

The main lake at St Lucia campus: a haven for walkers and bird-life alike

CHAPTER 2

BOOM TIMES

'GOOD LORD! DIDN'T YOU know? Moving to St Lucia is a University Legend!' With the war over, in 1945 the student magazine *Semper Floreat* wasn't about to let up on the senate. Such was the perceived lack of urgency that students joked that the move to St Lucia might take place by the 'spring of 2075'. Behind the scenes, though, it had been a very different reality, with university staff working tirelessly and against great odds financially to get construction moving.

Well-dressed picnickers in the early 1950s, on the site later occupied by the Abel Smith Lecture Theatre

During the first years of the war, relations between the senate and Premier Forgan Smith became rather tense, especially when he introduced legislation in 1941 that sought to control education from 'kindergarten through to university'. It didn't matter that JD Story had helped draft the Bill, as Story was forever being criticised internally for failing to comprehend that the University wasn't a branch of the public service. The academics were terrified of losing their self-determination, because under the new Act government nominees would have a majority on the senate. Strangely, though, they didn't complain, and it was left to the Student Union to protest. By October 1943 the University's relationship with Forgan Smith had improved enough for him to be welcomed on the senate as the 'university's friend', and after the death of Sir James W Blair in 1944, Forgan Smith was elected chancellor, going on to become one of the institution's greatest champions. At a degree ceremony in 1945 he dispelled any doubts about his perceived allegiance to the government, calling for 'complete freedom for university teaching staff and students to seek truth in discussion and research'.

JD Story, the first full-time vice-chancellor, 1955

After the war and due to a lack of manpower and materials, the state government's immediate concern was the funding of public housing and the state schools. Unfortunately, this meant that plans for university expansion came in a distant third. The original estimate of £500,000 for the first phase of building at St Lucia was now increased to £1,500,000. Despite this, Arts (with the exception of Mathematics), Commerce, Education and the library had moved to St Lucia by the end of 1948. Engineering was doing well enough to have expanded by 1949 and was even able to subdivide into three separate departments: Civil, Mechanical and Electrical. The economy was improving too, and with a new premier, Edward (Ned) Hanlon, at the helm the government was again in a position to offer more assistance, doubling its annual endowment to the University. Premier Hanlon officially opened the Main Building in 1949, and

The decorations in the Great Court were hand-carved in situ. Sculptor Theodore Muller at work in 1940.

Australian white ibises frequent the trees and parklands of the St Lucia campus.

Chemistry, Law and Mathematics moved to St Lucia. Geology was delayed until the following year.

Around this time, Vice-Chancellor JD Story started calling for a review of the original St Lucia concept designed by the Sydney architectural firm Hennessy, Hennessy and Co. After more than a decade there were many new issues that desperately needed addressing. He was especially worried that the Great Hall and many other construction projects had no funding drive to get them up and running. Many critics were openly questioning the wisdom of having a university that was described as being 'scattered all over the face of Brisbane'. As an administrator, JD Story has legendary status. Born in Scotland, he came to Queensland as a boy with his family and later won a scholarship to Brisbane Grammar, although he left school at fifteen when he was recommended by the headmaster for a position in the public service. After his job interview, it was noted that young Story was rather frail in build while possessing a brain stronger than his body. Known as 'old eagle' in university circles in his later years, he was a modest man who liked to ride the bus to work in George Street. 'More work, less argument' was one of his favourite sayings. He is reported to have abhorred 'petty meanness' although was renowned for being tight with money and secretive in controlling university finances. Although he had his detractors, he will be remembered as an energetic and astute man who steered the University successfully through the post-war explosion of enrolments and building projects. Despite having no university degree, education was his lifelong passion, and he steadfastly refused to accept an honorary degree when he retired. During his time as vice-chancellor, student numbers increased from 1,400 to 8,700 and the annual budget from £40,000 to £2 million.

Before the war the senate had allotted spots for the six colleges at St Lucia – Emmanuel, St John's, King's, St Leo's, Women's and Duchesne. The construction costs of each college were estimated at £40,000 and the senate agreed to lend £20,000 towards the building of each one. During the war the Student Union began to plan a non-denominational Union College at St Lucia, and from 1947 started operating a Union Hostel in Wickham Terrace, which the senate accepted as an affiliated college. For the time being, though, the senate baulked at the idea of giving the union land to build on at St Lucia. By 1954, and with nothing yet built, the government agreed to a £75,000 subsidy to each college, whose building costs had now increased to £150,000. King's began at St Lucia campus in 1954, Emmanuel moved in 1955 and St John's moved the following year. Cromwell (built by the Congregational churches in Queensland) took in its first students in June 1954. Meanwhile, the senate rejected plans

The Undergraduate Library in the mid-1950s. Before air-conditioning ducts and computers, the elegant fenestration of the Duhig Building could still be enjoyed, along with the open air.

Residents with the Vice-Rector (Students), Steve Foley, at St Leo's College, 2009. All the colleges offer tutorial assistance and a wide array of extra-curricular activities.

Student residents at Cromwell College gather round the Mr Whippy van, 1960s

for an International House even though many foreign students were attending the University after the war, under the Colombo Plan and the schemes of UNESCO and other world agencies. By the end of 1959, Women's and Duchesne had opened at St Lucia and work was about to begin on St Leo's. The graduation of the University's first Asian students restored the drive for an International House, which received its first students in February 1965 and was officially opened in June 1965. To date it has welcomed 4,000 students from around Australia and over ninety countries. Union College joined King's and Emmanuel on Upland Road, St Lucia, in 1965. Its design was praised for its use of Mt Coot-tha bluestone and superb views, but it was criticised by nearby residents who felt that the four-storey structure dominated the landscape. In June 1968 nearly two acres on the corner of Carmody Road and Walcott Street were made available for Grace College, which was built for Presbyterian and Methodist women, and was ready in 1970.

JD Story and the senate had other problems apart from the regular financial headaches. There was a perception in the community, stirred up by the media, that the University of Queensland was doing little to stimulate the intellectual and cultural life of the state and had a 'lofty indifference to the outside world'. Not surprisingly, these sorts of articles usually appeared in the press after Commemoration in April, when the students had annoyed the public with their pranks. JD Story saw the danger in this perception continuing and he ordered a public relations blitz, including some 'chatty' stories in the *University of Queensland Gazette* in the hope of promoting the more studious aspects of the University.

The PR campaign culminated in 1952 with the making of a film that could be shown to audiences around the state. In charge of the film's production was a photographer from the University who just happened to be named Ernie Hollywood. The film was a huge success and attracted good crowds wherever it screened, from Coolangatta to Cairns. With momentum swinging in the University's favour, JD Story then sent university staff out into the business world seeking donations from industry leaders and philanthropists. A series

Great Court, 1962, looking towards the Steele Building. Since then, a program of plantings has 'greened' the precinct.

Taking a break between lectures at one of the many cafés on the St Lucia campus

of public lectures was held in Brisbane and around the state to promote the University, and staff were encouraged to involve themselves in the local community to counteract the unfavourable publicity generated by the unruly behaviour of the students. In 1956 a senate meeting was filmed in colour and made into another film. The Duke of Edinburgh visited in March 1954, the Queen Mother in February 1958, and Princess Alexandra was given an honorary degree the following year, which gave the University a chance to show its students in a better light.

By 1955 the University of Queensland had become a victim of its own success. Student growth and academic expansion had placed the senate in an even greater financial dilemma, forcing JD Story to further narrow his building ambitions. He decided to first complete the physics building and make alterations to the tower in the Main Building to house the Faculty of Architecture. He then set up a subcommittee to begin raising money for a Great Hall, still clinging to the original Hennessy plan of attaching it at right angles to the Main Building's western edge to balance the library (the Duhig Building) located on the eastern wing. (This never happened and the space is now occupied by the Michie Building.) The Commonwealth government's involvement in the financial affairs of the University began in 1942 with scholarships and a commitment to maintain universities as a matter 'of national survival'. By 1946 it was providing 18 per cent of the University's income. From the beginning of 1958 a new system of Commonwealth, state and university-led funding developed. The Commonwealth, through the Murray Plan, offered a building grant of £1,500,000, which the state government under Premier Frank Nicklin enthusiastically matched. These might appear to be large sums of money, but in the context of the financial costs of the day they were not nearly enough to meet the huge bills required for the University to continue expanding at St Lucia, let alone the costs of the recommended sixty-five new academic positions to be created at the University that same year. The only finished structures at St Lucia in 1958 were the Main Building and those for Chemistry (the Steele Building), Geology (the Richards Building) and Physics (the Parnell Building). To complete the original half-circle Hennessy concept, the Biological Sciences block and the Great Hall were needed. There was no money for either. Undeterred, JD Story scaled things back even further. Building beyond the half-circle was reduced and excluded the popular freestone veneers that were so expensive. Traditional and classic architecture was abandoned to make way for styles and designs that better accommodated the more cost-effective materials available for construction after the war. Funding from the Commonwealth was on a triennial basis and involved a mountain of paperwork, so planning had to be meticulous. There was a debate about the idea of using space in the Great Court for two buildings to save money; however, on this issue JD Story wouldn't budge, insisting the area remain 'sacrosanct'. The Biological Sciences building (the Goddard Building) was completed in stages, which in 1959 allowed the entry of Agriculture, then Zoology in 1960, and Botany and Entomology in 1961. Prime Minister Robert Menzies made his first visit in 1961 and received an honorary degree. His presence on campus cemented a new era of Commonwealth funding.

The vice-chancellor's role changed significantly during the boom period. It was accepted that JD Story's 'honorary' position would be followed by a full-time paid executive officer in the pattern of other universities. The 1957 University

The concrete brutalism of the just completed JD Story Building was in keeping with the civic architectural trend of the early 1960s.

Fred Schonell, c. 1950

Eleanor Schonell, c. 1950

Grace College, an all-female college, provides both academic and social activities for its students, 2009.

Act made a provision for such an appointment. Professor Fred Schonell took over as vice-chancellor from 1 March 1960 – the year of the Golden Jubilee celebrations. Schonell had held chairs in Education at the universities of Wales and Birmingham, before being appointed foundation Professor of Education at the University of Queensland, where he became the leading expert in his field internationally. The 'old eagle' JD Story remained on the senate until 1963 and was chairman of the Finance Committee. He died in 1966. It is worth noting that he completed his twenty-two years as vice-chancellor without moving his office from George Street to St Lucia. Professor Schonell, who was knighted in 1962, had a different personality from Story, the former more outgoing and worldly, as comfortable in the company of royalty and overseas dignitaries as he was with the man or woman in the street. The one thing both educators had in common was a belief that the University was established to serve all Queenslanders. Schonell was a strong advocate of Asian studies and fought the Faculty of Arts for their inclusion, and for training courses for university teachers. He was also seen as a champion of people with learning difficulties and devoted great energy to what was known at the time as 'sub-normal education'. His wife, Eleanor, an educational psychologist, achieved international recognition for designing a test for dyslexia and for her work with cerebral palsy children. Like her husband, she was known for her caring and humane approach to people from all walks of life, especially the disadvantaged. Together they developed standardised ways to test the academic abilities of children, and both wrote textbooks that sold millions of copies.

Under Professor Fred Schonell, the University consciously set out to do more entertaining and wining and dining to involve the business community. The hallowed doors of the University were thrown open to television cameras for the first time and Schonell set up weekly press conferences. In his nine years in charge, student numbers grew from 8,700 to 15,000, including a rise in the number of female students, of which Schonell was a strong advocate.

Princess Alexandra and Chancellor Sir Albert Axon arriving at UQ on the occasion of her receiving an honorary degree, in 1959, at the centenary of the foundation of Queensland as a separate colony from New South Wales.

Students in the recently opened Abel Smith Lecture
Theatre, 1968

In the early 1960s it was thought that Queensland had one of the lowest enrolments of women students in the world. With some encouragement from Schonell, by 1966 women accounted for one-quarter of the students studying science. (And they had also won the right to wear slacks to lectures, as long as the head of the department approved it.) Over a decade later, women accounted for over 40 per cent of the student body.

Schonell regularly phoned the *Courier-Mail* and the ABC to give them news about things that were going on at the University. Under his leadership, the University appointed its first public relations officer, Tom Drake. This was also a time when student radicalism was on the rise, with the Vietnam War and conscription for military service changing the political landscape. In March 1963 the introduction of identity cards for students was likened to George Orwell's novel *1984*. The threat of a Big Brother–like denial of people's liberty turned out to be a slight overreaction, and the hysteria whipped up was blamed on the left-wing radicals who were labelled 'unwashed crackpots' by the more conservative students. Drugs were starting to become a problem on campus, and the *Sunday Mail* reported in 1963 that a quarter of the students were under the influence of marijuana during exam time. How the newspaper

The imposing Medical School at Herston in 1959, adjacent to the Royal Brisbane Hospital complex. It was opened in 1939 and renamed the Mayne Medical School in 1996.

Students and patients at the Dentistry School in Turbot Street in the city in 1964. The long-awaited new Oral Health Centre is to be built next to the Medical School at Herston.

established this statistic was never revealed. Rather than trying to stamp out drugs by calling in the police, Schonell increased student counselling services as a way of dealing with the problem, and in 1968 distributed pamphlets during Orientation week called *Drugs and You* on the dangers of hallucinogenic drugs such as LSD.

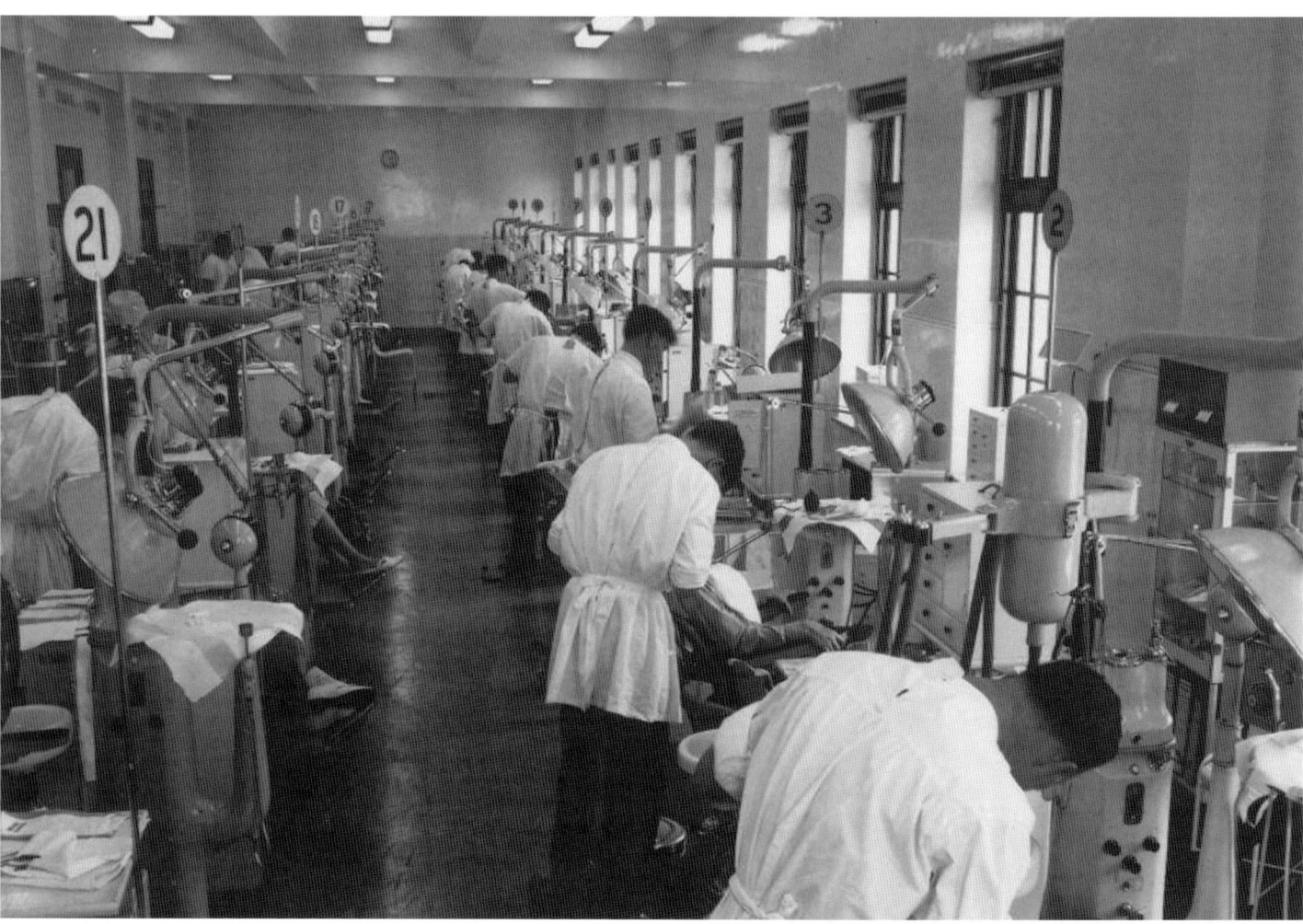

There was also the continuing problem of student behaviour during Commemoration celebrations, which had moved beyond the prank stage and now involved brawls with police in the city streets. The issue of the Vietnam War and conscription made the situation explicitly political. Twenty-two students were locked up in the watch-house and charged with disorderly conduct after one demonstration. When staff members were accused of being among the agitators, the situation looked to be getting out of control. It was rumoured that Special Branch police had infiltrated the University to spy on students and suspected communists. Schonell's stance was that the University offered people a chance to voice their opinions but that it should be done through the proper channels and without violence. He was helped in these difficult days by the appointment of the University's first deputy vice-chancellor, Professor Hartley Teakle. Teakle's role increased enormously when Schonell fell ill with Hodgkin's disease in 1968 and he presided over the University following Schonell's death in 1969. With tensions continuing to escalate on campus, his was not an enviable position, and his services to the University were acknowledged in the naming of the Hartley Teakle Building in June 1971.

The lack of private donations was still hampering the University's development. On the death of Dr Mayne in 1939 and his sister Mary Emelia in 1940, the University had been bequeathed property in the city, including the Brisbane Arcade in Queen Street, which was immediately put to work generating an income for the Faculty of Medicine. Apart from that, there were very few benefactors, although Albert Axon, who became chancellor in 1957, used his business connections to start raising funds for the Great Hall. During this period Archbishop James Duhig, who was on the senate for nearly fifty years, made

The St Lucia campus from the air, 1960. The original buildings of the Great Court are all in place and excavations are under way for science and engineering buildings.

The first UQ computer, manufactured by General Electric, is treated with appropriate respect, 1962.

numerous donations to the University, including the generous gift of seismology equipment to Geology and Mineralogy, and the Rockefeller Foundation gave over £20,000 for the Marine Research Station on Heron Island in the Great Barrier Reef. (The University now assumes full responsibility for this research station, as well as others on the Low Isles off Port Douglas in Far North Queensland and on North Stradbroke Island in Moreton Bay.)

In 1959 land was allocated for Staff House and nearly eight years later a Commonwealth loan was used to furnish the completed building. By 1961 the physical education building, later named the Connell Building and located between Circular Drive and the Brisbane River, was finished. The first-year science building, now known as the Priestley Building, and the Social Sciences Building were both constructed outside Circular Drive and were ready for students in 1964. The Abel Smith Lecture Theatre, named after Queensland governor Sir Henry Abel Smith, was built between them and opened in February 1966. Under the Commonwealth government's Murray Plan, the first stage of the Student Union building was ready for use in 1961. In 1968 plans were approved for the Union Theatre (later renamed the Schonell Theatre) and an extension to the Union Complex. The JD Story Administration Building – built away from the Forgan Smith Building to relieve the already considerable stress on teaching space there – was finished in early October 1965 and nearly 200 administration staff promptly moved in. In 1961 the Anatomy building (the Otto Hirschfeld Building) came into use and was immediately overcrowded. The Biochemistry building (the John Hines Building) was dubbed the 'cheapest and nastiest' of all the new buildings, although some thought the Social Sciences Building deserving of this unflattering title (a later

contender was the Abel Smith Lecture Theatre, labelled the 'pizza hut' by some). The Physiology building (the Sir William MacGregor Building) was available for use by students and lecturers in 1964. Chancellor MacGregor would have been proud to learn that, of all the new buildings in this period, Physiology was considered the most spacious and best equipped.

Women's softball practice on the oval behind the Student Union complex and the Social Sciences Building in 1960. The main campus is surrounded by sporting ovals that were flooded in 1974.

With the building of the Eleanor Schonell Bridge, staff and students from the inner southern suburbs and beyond no longer have to catch the Dutton Park ferry.

Beyond St Lucia, the acquisition of a long lease over an old silver-lead mine at Indooroopilly in 1951 was a great asset to the University for future generations of engineering students. In May 1966 a new Clinical Sciences block became available at Royal Brisbane Hospital, inspiring the Dean, Professor Douglas Gordon, to famously comment that the Medical School had moved out of the 'dungeon stage' of its development. Veterinary Science had a new building (the Seddon Building) ready for use in 1961. Less fortunate was Dentistry. The Dental Hospital and College was first opened in 1941 at Turbot Street, and since the post-war explosion in enrolments the Faculty of Dentistry had lobbied the senate to relocate to St Lucia. Promises were made and then retracted. By the early 1960s conditions at Turbot Street were described as slum-like and, despite an expensive renovation (costing up to £800,000) a few years later, the complaints about overcrowding continued. A degree in Dentistry now took five years, instead of three, and more than 300 students were crammed into the facilities. Morale in Engineering, however, was boosted when new Civil Engineering laboratories were ready at St Lucia in 1961. Stage one of the Mechanical Engineering building (the Mansergh Shaw Building) was completed in 1964. Professor Sydney Prentice, of Electrical Engineering, who had spent the best part of a decade travelling back and forth between St Lucia and George Street, where he'd even worked out of an old hut, finally moved to St Lucia in 1965. Despite all this frantic building activity, sufficient money couldn't be found to erect the Great Hall, even though there had been widespread community support for the appeal conducted in association with the 1960 Jubilee. In August 1967 Old Government House still housed

Pharmacy and Education. Some major off-campus projects were completed in the mid-1960s. These included the conversion of two floors of the Mater Hospital at South Brisbane for teaching surgery, stage one of the Pastoral Veterinary Centre at Goondiwindi, an extension of the Medical School at Herston, and improved facilities for Moggill Farm.

A degree ceremony at the Brisbane City Hall for UQ's Golden Jubilee in 1960, the palm trees behind the senior academic staff adding a note of subtropical informality. At that time UQ did not have a suitable venue for degree ceremonies.

Prime Minister Robert Menzies receiving his honorary degree from Chancellor Axon in 1961. Menzies, a graduate of the University of Melbourne, boosted federal funding for universities, which at the time were still dependent on state government grants and student fees for most of their income.

In 1964 Mining and Metallurgical Engineering, Pharmacy, Music and parts of Mechanical Engineering and Education were still at George Street and Microbiology was awaiting relocation from Herston. Despite the huge amount of land available at St Lucia, it was clear that the University was running out of quality building space. Some argued that new buildings could easily be accommodated on the huge tracts of land situated below the flood plain, which had been set aside for use as sporting fields, an argument that was resisted fiercely and then laid to rest when the devastating floods of 1974 caused nearly $1 million damage.

In 1964 the University needed £4 million to balance its budget but had fallen £200,000 short. In order to survive, several rather unpalatable solutions were offered to the senate. The first was to introduce student quotas, which was immediately rejected as being against the principles of a people's university. The second was to set up a second university in Brisbane to ease the strain on the existing university. A few years previously, in its Golden Jubilee year, the University had established a college in Townsville, later to become James Cook University, as a way to lessen the burden on the St Lucia campus. More University Centres were established in the 1970s, at Toowoomba, Rockhampton, Cairns and Mackay, to enhance the support offered to the University's many external students. Meanwhile, another possible solution to the lack of finances that was to frustrate vice-chancellors for the next twenty years was to secure a better deal for Queensland under the Universities Commission. Queensland was still seen as the poor cousin to its southern rivals and as such was the lowest funded of all the Australian states. In 1969 the Universities Commission refused the senate's application to provide funds for air-conditioning, although the Commission had no qualms about providing millions to Sydney and Melbourne so their universities could be heated. The estimated expenditure for the University of Queensland in that year was nearly $15 million, an increase of over $2 million on the previous year.

Between 1957 and 1966 the University expanded by one thousand students per year. Of course, other universities around Australia were expanding too and this meant that the poaching of staff was common. The days of staff loyalty were over. Some of the early administration staff retired at about this time (a few who had joined the staff as teenagers from school had been there for an incredible fifty years). It wasn't just the political landscape that was changing rapidly. Advances in technology meant that money had to be found for expensive equipment, including the University's first electron microscope, to be used for cancer research, and a digital computer installed by General Electric in 1962. By April 1967, university demand for computing capacity

The computer room in 1962, housing UQ's first computer

Professors Webster, Bennett (University of Sydney) and Prentice (left to right) inspect the proposed site of the computer centre. For much of its history the St Lucia campus has resembled a building site.

The University Squadron on parade inside the Great
Court in 1960. The Squadron fell victim to federal
government defence spending cutbacks in 1973.

had grown dramatically, and a better computer system was required. A new computer supporting eight simultaneous users soon filled the floor of the Computer Centre, which occupied the basement of what is now known as the Prentice Building. The same computing power is available many times

Matriculation ceremony in the university gym in the Connell Building, 1968

St Lucia campus, 1966. Under construction are the additional floors on the top of the Duhig Building, while the site of the future Michie Building is a carpark. At this time the Great Court still commanded the land in front of it before the addition of Mayne Hall.

over in even the humblest of today's laptops. A new research-driven university planned for Mt Gravatt put pressure on the University of Queensland to update its technology and focus more on research. In 1960 Electrical Engineering installed a one-million-volt transformer, while the Department of Physics landed a contract from the American air force for space research. New technology hadn't yet replaced the need for libraries and books. In the 1960s the University had 300,000 print volumes to handle the needs of 16,000 students. Today the University has fourteen libraries with 2.5 million print volumes, along with 18,000 computers (computer access accounts for 80 per cent of library usage), networked databases, electronic books, microfilm and pictorial collections and videos.

In the 1960s staff benefits also improved, ushering in a golden age for those with dreams of academia. In May 1962 the senate agreed to the appointment of academic staff until age sixty-five, subject to a probationary period. This was later increased to seventy for a time, provided the staff member was in good health, so basically it was tenure for life. Staff had previously worked under contracts of five or seven years. By this time they had also acquired the right to apply for study leave after six years. Matriculation – the University was still responsible for the entrance exam – was also tightened again. From 1965 all faculties required five passes at Senior level. At about the same time the senate was notified of the formation of a University of Queensland Club (informally known as the Staff Club), which brought up the issue of a kindergarten for the children of academic and administrative staff. Since the late 1950s the Commonwealth government, under the Murray Plan, had stressed the need for a happy and contented staff and had urged the creation of facilities to make this possible.

Unfortunately for the University, happy times weren't around the corner. Some staff were joining with the students on political issues, especially later when it came to the democratic right to march and the heavy-handed tactics of the police who broke up demonstrations. The conservative leanings of the post-war construction focus and education boom were about to be replaced by a tidal wave of discontent fuelled by sex, drugs and rock'n'roll and the Vietnam

Research under way in the clear waters off Heron Island, 2009. Some overseas students are attracted to UQ because of the possibility of undertaking research on the Great Barrier Reef.

UQ Union's business manager Ray Thorne (centre) explains the Schonell Theatre's renovation to biomedical students Susan Scott and Elliot Lambert, 2004.

War. The move to St Lucia would be complete in 1972, but there would be no time to sit back and enjoy the magnitude of the achievement. The next phase of the University's development would feature heated clashes and escalating tensions between the establishment and a student body demanding change. The principles on which the University had been founded were about to be tested in ways the early academic pioneers could never have imagined.

The Brisbane Customs House was purchased by UQ in the mid-1990s and restored with public donations.

CHAPTER 3

GROWING PAINS

Mayne Hall (the originally envisaged Great Hall) was
a long time in the planning, opening in 1973. Finally
graduation ceremonies could be held on campus rather
than at the Brisbane City Hall.

'WHAT IS THE ROLE of the university within society?' The question was shouted at members of the senate when they were physically confronted by a sit-in of students in June 1969. The question was difficult for them to answer, because the University was fast becoming a battleground for social and political change as opposed to a centre for higher learning. The following month a 'nude male' paraded on the roof of the library. The so-called erotica display was organised by the Revolutionary Socialist Students' Alliance as a sign of sexual liberation. A nude ballet at the Schonell Theatre would shock everyone a few years later.

Mayne Hall was a public venue for musical performance from the 1970s to 2001. Its redevelopment as an art gallery in the new century left the University without a musical performance space.

UQ clubs and societies recruit during Orientation Week at the St Lucia campus, much as they did in medieval universities.

The senate's reaction to the student sit-in was passive and accommodating, which no doubt helped defuse a potentially dangerous situation. The senate allowed the student leader and two others to air their views for ten minutes each. Afterwards, the senate went ahead with plans for a seminar in the Great Court that had been organised previously to give students an opportunity to voice their opinions on a wide range of reforms, including that students should have a greater say in the University's decision-making process. According to the *Courier-Mail*, about 4,000 people attended the seminar on a chilly Brisbane afternoon, and all the recommendations put forward during the heated debates were eventually adopted by the University (albeit over a period of many years). The senate in 1969 even allowed the students a voice in the selection of the new vice-chancellor, after the death of Sir Fred Schonell.

As for the erotica display, the senate decided on disciplinary proceedings for those involved but didn't think it necessary to involve the police (even the press considered it a non-event), although larger-than-life state politician Russ Hinze, later to be known as the 'Minister for Everything', wasn't about to miss the chance to score a political point. He vowed to make the University 'a place of intellectual and religious freedom for all, not one of licence and unrestrained vulgarity'. Perhaps stirred up by Hinze, another state politician made the astonishing claim under parliamentary privilege that there were twenty-one cases of venereal disease in the Department of English, and then demanded to know how many pregnancies there had been at St Lucia that year.

With a greater say in how things were being run at the University, the students' attention now shifted from campus politics to the changing political landscape in the outside world. In May 1969, during Labour Day celebrations, anti-war protestors, including students from the University, some wearing helmets emblazoned with the words 'Viet Cong', created havoc in the Exhibition Grounds after gate-crashing an official function. However, it was not until the May 1970 Vietnam Moratorium that the 'New Left' student movement became a force to be reckoned with on campus. The new vice-chancellor, Professor Zelman Cowen, warned that lectures would not be cancelled, but then in an extraordinary gesture he said that they could be rescheduled. Rebelling students erected tents in the Great Court and taunted the senate during the May days of protest to come and take them down.

Zelman Cowen was born in Melbourne and went to Oxford as a Rhodes scholar where he studied civil law. He became dean of the Faculty of Law at the University of Melbourne, and subsequently the vice-chancellor at the University of New England. By the time of his appointment as vice-chancellor of the University of Queensland,

Professor Zelman Cowen accepting a cheque for $10,000 from the Alumni Association to be used for Mayne Hall furnishings, November 1972. Left to right: Kevin See, Len Fisher, Zelman Cowen, Jim Ritchie.

Alumni Court, between the Goddard and Parnell buildings, is a quiet haven for students and staff.

The card catalogue in the Main Library (now part of the Social Sciences and Humanities Library) in 1973, which gave way to a computer catalogue in 1988. Online access to the collection itself was provided progressively during the 1990s.

he was considered by many to be one of the leading constitutional lawyers in the world. If ever there was a man for the times it was Cowen. He would need all his diplomatic skills as he faced one crisis after another in his new position.

In early September the headquarters of the Queensland University Regiment were damaged by political radicals, and this was followed by what the *Courier-Mail* described as a 'near riot' when the first secretary of the South Vietnamese embassy in Canberra visited the University. Police clashed violently with students, and newspaper headlines the next day called it a 'Day of Shame'. As an inquiry into the incident was being launched, tents were again erected in the Great Court, this time with the help of some University lecturers, and the area was temporarily renamed the 'People's Park'. The senate decided on a referendum to gauge the mood of the campus, and discovered that over three-quarters of the staff and students were opposed to the tents. Again, they were taken down and disciplinary action ordered against those involved.

A strong advocate of civil liberties, Zelman Cowen made his views clear on student behaviour on campus: the senate had no desire to enforce censorship as long as people acted within the law. He backed the students on many issues.

The jacarandas on campus herald preparations for second semester exams.

The new Staff House in 1968. In the early years students were not allowed to use the facilities. They can now have a drink or a meal at Staff House in the company of a member of the University of Queensland Club.

Bounded on two sides by the Brisbane River, the lower parts of the St Lucia campus, as well as Fairfield/Yeronga on the other side of the river, were among areas inundated by the 1974 flood. The colleges in the middle ground were just above the flood line.

Calls to ban the set texts deemed offensive by the Community Standards Association for first-year English students were resisted. When in February 1977 the state government began to contemplate new legislation to dissolve the Student Union, Cowen stood by the union and fought for its rights. He declared from the outset his welcome of criticism but his disdain for chaos and destruction. Cowen was personally abused many times, but he was known for his self-control in such situations. He also stood up for a member of staff who was a known agitator but also a respected teacher, and made sure that the man didn't lose his job during the days of protest when there were many in the senate calling for him to be made an example of.

A visit by the governor-general Sir Paul Hasluck to open the Schonell Theatre about two weeks after the 'Day of Shame' saw another demonstration. Cowen was true to his word and the senate issued suspensions. There was also a criminal conviction after an arrest, although Cowen denied that anyone from the University had called the police. The next flashpoint was the visit of the South African rugby team, the Springboks, in the winter of 1971. The Queensland government took the unprecedented step of declaring a state of emergency, after anti-apartheid demonstrators in Sydney two weeks previously had invaded the pitch and torn down the goalposts. Premier Joh

The introduction of the CityCat by the Brisbane City Council in the mid-1990s meant that staff and students could get from areas such as New Farm, Bulimba and the CBD to UQ via the river.

Prime Minister Gough Whitlam at a Health Conference at the UQ campus in 1975. UQ alumnus Llew Edwards (second from left), was the then state member of parliament for Ipswich and the Minister for Health.

Bjelke-Petersen wasn't about to allow the same thing to happen in Brisbane, and he brought in police from all over the state to protect the South Africans when they played the Wallabies at the Exhibition Grounds. University students joined with the trade unions to march through the city on the day of the match. Over 2,000 students staged a sit-in and took over the Student Union building for the duration of the Springboks' visit. A demonstration after the game outside the Tower Mill Motel on Wickham Terrace, where the Springboks were staying, featured one of the bloodiest confrontations in Brisbane's history, as police arrested hundreds of students, including future premier and University of Queensland alumnus Peter Beattie, who later said that it was this incident that sparked his interest in politics. Police were accused of ripping off their shoulder badges before they charged into the crowd of students so they wouldn't be recognised. Students were beaten with batons and fists by police officers, one of whom was held hostage in the old Trade Union Building until negotiators secured his release. Afterwards, the students and some supportive staff called a strike at the University. The vice-chancellor warned that striking staff would lose their pay, and about 4,500 students were reported to be missing from lectures. Cowen sought the cooperation of police commissioner Ray Whitrod during the rolling protests, as people were questioning why the police weren't more involved on campus. This was in response to criticism levelled at him for 'condoning violence' by showing a level of tolerance towards the students.

In 1978 it was alleged that a member of the police Special Branch, masquerading as a student, had been placed on campus to collect information. The University was incensed and demanded that no such action should take place without the University's permission. The police commissioner took the opposite view and quietly ignored the vice-chancellor. The senate had never denied that students on campus were taking drugs, but, rather than tackling the problem by calling in the Drug Squad, it was decided that it was a matter that could be dealt with by the Health Service, student counsellors and the chaplains in the various colleges. In later years it was revealed that Special Branch police were spying on university students well before 1978. The Special Branch was disbanded and its files shredded after the Fitzgerald Inquiry into police corruption ended in 1989.

When Gough Whitlam swept into power at the end of 1972, the Labor government ended conscription and withdrew Australian troops from Vietnam, which caused jubilation among the students and had a noticeable calming effect on campus. However, it has been argued in some circles that to a large extent it was the introduction of the semester system in 1974 that killed off enthusiasm for further protests. The semester system introduced more regular assessment, which meant that more energy had to be devoted to studying to ensure good grades. Racism, though, was still seen as an issue worth drawing attention to. In July 1972 masked students representing the Black Panthers, the famous American civil rights group, stormed the Senate Room to demand black rights and an end to racism on campus. They had planned to disrupt the senate meeting but arrived on the wrong day, barging in instead on the startled Library Committee. In November 1975 many students marched in protest at the dismissal of Gough Whitlam, and in July 1976 they marched with students and teachers from other tertiary institutions calling for more generous student allowances.

Student protesters march against the war in Vietnam in 1970. Many protest marches took place on campus as the Bjelke-Petersen government attempted to hamper, and then banned, street marches in the city.

The first organ recital at Mayne Hall in 1976, with Robert Boughen as the organist

When Cowen was offered the role of governor-general in 1977 after the premature retirement of Sir John Kerr (who had controversially dismissed the federal Labor government under Gough Whitlam), he was given leave of absence to prepare for his new responsibilities. He left behind no fewer than seventeen buildings completed during his period in office, including Mayne Hall (the originally planned Great Hall), the new venue for graduation ceremonies. Considering the University's financial strains during the 1970s, it was a miracle that anything had been built at all. The Biological Sciences Library and the Commerce Building (later the Chamberlain Building) and the Chemical Engineering Building had been completed and occupied, and progress had been made on the sandstone façade of the Michie Building. Mayne Hall, designed by Robin Gibson, was finally built for $600,000, with companies Myer and BP contributing generously for the furnishing of the building, while the Alumni Association (founded in 1967) also played a huge role in this, later putting a further $20,000 towards the costs of an organ to be manufactured in Germany.

Cowen helped streamline the university administration, and he also added the Department of Fine Arts to the campus (something that Archbishop Duhig had for years tried unsuccessfully to achieve) and developed Mayne Hall as a concert hall for all Queenslanders to enjoy. According to the *Courier-Mail*, in 1969 the buildings on the St Lucia campus had to date cost $30 million. Cowen admitted that the University was overcrowded and that the Law School accommodation was inadequate. Buildings were described by one public servant as a 'muck up' and a 'hotch-potch' of differing architectural styles and designs. A new master plan was ordered, which led to the partial closure of Circular Drive and the creation of the much-loved pedestrian precinct of today. Under Cowen, the plan for the area in front of the Forgan Smith Building was to include buildings at both ends and another pedestrian precinct in-between. JD Story would have been turning in his grave, as this was another 'sacrosanct' area. The senate knew the legendary vice-chancellor's views on this, but the University had run out of space and such superb building land had become a rarity.

Members of the UQ Cricket Club played an Indian provincial team, July 2009.

Rhyl Shepherd (later Hinwood) carving the grotesque of her predecessor, sculptor Ted Muller, in 1981

In 1969 the senate's main business was financing the running of the University, which was about $13 million per year at the time. The University relied on income from three streams: the Commonwealth through the Universities Commission, the state government and university fees. The problem was that the Universities Commission seemed to favour the southern universities at the expense of Queensland (and couldn't explain why). Another problem was the state government's participation in the process. When the state government cried poor – which happened on a few occasions in the 1960s – fees were increased to make up the funding shortfall. Cowen's tenure as vice-chancellor was like those before him: in both boom times and depressions the situation was always the same – the University was in a critical financial position. Cowen pointed to staff salary increases as one of the main drains on resources, and he even talked about borrowing money for the Great Hall to be finished. This was not well received. In 1972 fees under Cowen had risen by nearly 30 per cent, among the highest in Australia, and he called for nationally funded universities as a means of lifting the burden on the state. He got his wish when new prime minister Gough Whitlam told the state premiers that from 1974 fees would be abolished and the federal government would be assuming responsibility for universities and other tertiary institutions.

With Whitlam's dismissal and the political crisis that divided the country, the University of Queensland ended up in even more financial trouble. Suddenly the old system of triennial planning and funding didn't seem so bad after all. By 1978 the University was spending almost 90 per cent of its income on wages and salaries. Quotas on student numbers were introduced in 1975 on all first-year courses to ease funding pressure, with the University of Queensland the last of the established universities to do this. In the 1960s quotas had reluctantly been introduced in Medicine and Veterinary Science. Determined to remain a 'people's university', the senate preserved the open-door policy for every other faculty, although it was mentioned that quotas did allow for better control over the University's size and shape. In 1971, when the senate resolved to toughen matriculation requirements, the University was accused of placing research work ahead of first-degree students. Immediately, first-year enrolments fell to below 3,000. Elitism had raised its ugly head again, some complained. With

Approaching the entrance to the Social Sciences and Humanities Library (formerly the Undergraduate Library) along the Forgan Smith Building cloister. Café Merlo was created in the old bag racks section of the library and spills out into the Great Court.

The refectory area was a popular gathering place
for students in the mid-1970s, when they were more
concerned with politics than fashion.

Students at the Commerce (later Chamberlain)
Building, 1975. By the mid-1970s student dress had
become much more informal, especially for males, who
had abandoned shorts and long socks for stubbies and
thongs.

A lunch-hour concert by the Queensland Symphony Orchestra in the University Music Shell, located in the undercroft of the Physiology lecture theatres, in 1971. In 1985 the space was converted into the Physiology Refectory.

the introduction at the beginning of 1972 of the Radford Scheme of school-based assessment, the University was finally relieved of the responsibility for the Senior matriculation examination.

In June 1975 a proposal from the Sports and Physical Recreation Association for the establishment of a fully licensed club premises was approved. By October 1976 the famous 'Rec' Club was ready for operation and set to become arguably the most popular institution in University history. (Today the Red Room in the Student Union complex is the place to go.) With the beer and wine flowing, and community radio station Triple Zed broadcasting alternative music that had been ignored (or banned) by the FM commercial stations, the campus social scene exploded into life and had a distinctive rebellious edge. Debates on campus became heated over the funding for Triple Zed, which relied on the Student Union for its income, and over whether its perceived 'left-wing' leanings were truly representative of the student body. The radicals squared off with the conservatives, and although that battle petered out in the late 1970s it was to raise its head again in the late 1980s, with protests and brawls with police that brought national media attention. In 1988 the newly installed Student Union executive, accompanied by security guards, forcibly evicted two Triple Zed graveyard shift announcers. An emergency broadcast message was sent out from Mt Coot-tha warning listeners of the *coup d'etat*. Hundreds of supporters rallied to the cause. They took back the station and occupied the union offices until police hauled them out. The subsequent violence on campus went on for weeks as the legality of a student petition seeking the resignation of the union executive travelled laboriously through the courts,

St Lucia was once considered too far away from the city centre to justify moving the campus there from its George Street headquarters. Today, with much improved public transport links, visitors, staff and students can get to the University from the CBD within ten minutes by bus.

The finished carving of Ted Muller, depicted with his mallet and chisel, is located at the western end of the Forgan Smith Building, facing the Great Court.

eventually ending up in front of Justice Paul de Jersey in the Supreme Court of Queensland.

In the end, Triple Zed moved to the nearby suburb of Toowong and then Fortitude Valley closer to the city, but once off-campus it was never again able to raise the political passion of students, and had to seek subscriptions from other sections of the community. Civil liberty demonstrations in 1977 brought further skirmishes between police and members of the university. It was illegal to march in Queensland without a permit (and permits were never granted), so to protest meant committing a crime. Under the conservative National–Liberal Coalition, life in Queensland was different from that of other states in Australia, as the new vice-chancellor was about to find out.

The James and Mary Emelia Mayne Centre,
formerly Mayne Hall

CHAPTER 4

AGE

OF

RESEARCH

Professor Brian Wilson at the 75th anniversary
celebrations at Old Government House, 1985

'THIS IS YOUR CAPTAIN speaking: Welcome to Queensland. Please turn your watches back one hour – and one hundred years!' The year was 1978. On board an Ansett flight to Brisbane was Belfast-born astrophysicist Professor Brian Wilson, who was arriving for a formal interview for the position of vice-chancellor at the University of Queensland.

Professor Wilson had visited Australia on two occasions in the 1960s, for a cosmic rays conference in Tasmania and, a few years later, as project scientist for the first Canadian-built rocket to be fired at Woomera in South Australia. Now he looked out the window as the airline passengers laughed at the pilot's remark. He recalled the advertisement for the position, which had included the comment that the successful applicant could pick bananas from the veranda of the vice-chancellor's residence.

On arrival he was impressed by the style and situation of the campus, and was overwhelmed by the friendliness and 'obvious quality' of the academic staff he met over the next couple of days. As he chatted to them, he was surprised to learn that the Dean of Medicine, responsible for the largest medical school in Australia, had only limited control over his budget. The academic management processes at the University surprised him. When he asked others who they were responsible to, he heard a variety of answers: the head of a department, the dean, the Board, or the vice-chancellor. Obviously, the question was unusual and unexpected. Wilson, who had come to Queensland following senior administrative appointments at the University of Calgary and Simon Fraser University in Canada, had been used to more decentralised, flexible organisation, with responsibility devolved to individuals. He was impressed, however, with the administrative support structure, which seemed clear-cut and well understood. But there was a much larger issue: everyone he spoke to expressed concern about the overall funding situation.

When offered the position, Professor Wilson decided that the opportunity to work in a large and well-regarded institution, with a broad range of professional disciplines, was a challenge he could not pass up. Besides, he thought, there was hardly a university in the world that didn't have problems with funding. He took up his appointment on 1 January 1979. Things did not get off to a good start. The banana tree at his new residence turned out to be diseased and had to be removed without delay! Much more important was his discovery that the Universities Council had been underfunding the University for a decade, to the tune of about $10 million in 1979 alone, when compared with the allocation to the University of Melbourne, which had comparable numbers of students and similar study programs. He learned later that the University was seen as culpable through the 1970s for regularly exceeding its student quotas (on which the Commonwealth grants were based). The University had introduced an 'open door' policy, offering places to all academically qualified students who applied. (With Griffith University not yet open, this policy reflected a reasonable response to meet increased student demand, allowing the proportion of Queensland school leavers wanting access to university courses to increase towards Australian levels.) A bureaucrat in Canberra allegedly commented: 'If Queensland can take them in, let them pay for them!'

Wilson, who completed an Honours degree in physics at Queen's University in Belfast and received his PhD from the National University of Ireland, following studies at the Dublin Institute for Advanced Studies, decided that his first task

Carvings of sulphur-crested cockatoos overlooking the Great Court

Staff members arrayed by discipline to advise newly enrolling science students in the early 1980s

was to get a better deal for the University. He found the perception of his coming from a 'backwater' like Queensland hard to take when he travelled to Canberra to talk with Universities Council officers, feeling that he was being treated like a 'new boy' who 'did not understand the situation'. Within a few years, however,

with the establishment of the federal Department of Employment and Training
under Labor Minister John Dawkins, which took over the Council's responsibility
for university funding, and made objective evaluations of the system, the
'situation' was resolved.

Communications racks in the Computer Centre, 1984,
when the number of desktop computers connected to
the university network was in the order of hundreds.
Today more than 20,000 are on UQnet, which connects
all the University sites.

UQ's experimental mine and the Julius Kruttschnitt Mineral Research Centre are located in the inner Brisbane residential suburb of Indooroopilly.

The massive changes to the education system in this period, known colloquially as the 'Dawkins Revolution', started with the introduction of a $250 higher education administrative charge in 1987. The effect of the charge was immediate: total enrolments at the University fell by 500. In December 1987 the federal government released its Higher Education Policy 'Green Paper', proposing sweeping changes to the structure of higher education in Australia that involved dismantling the binary system of universities and colleges of advanced education. In preparation for the changes, the University of Queensland would sponsor the university colleges of southern and central Queensland, at Toowoomba and Rockhampton respectively, as they moved towards university status. The University would also play a role in the development of Northern Territory University where it had a college. (The Queensland Agricultural College and the University of Queensland consolidation in January 1990 also resulted from the dismantling of the binary system. The consolidation resulted in a new campus, now known as UQ Gatton, located about 90 kilometres west of Brisbane, giving the University a strong leadership role in agricultural science.) It was the biggest change in higher education since the Commonwealth intervention in the university system following the Murray Report in 1957.

In 1988 a 'White Paper' by Dawkins signalled more significant changes in Australian higher education. The threat of the reintroduction of student fees eliminated by Whitlam in 1974 provoked widespread concern in the community, especially among academics and university administrators, as did the possibility of a graduate tax. In 1989 the Hawke government introduced delayed tuition fees under the guise of the Higher Education Contribution

Scheme (HECS). Fees had to be paid back once graduates were earning at a particular income level, continuing the shift towards the user-pays principle of higher education that had been foreshadowed by the establishment of the privately funded Bond University on the Gold Coast in 1987. Demand had outstripped supply and people were now prepared to pay for quality higher education.

Women's College nestling among the jacarandas and eucalypts between the lakes and the Brisbane River

King's College and St Leo's College rugby teams play for the Francis and Kassulke Cup, donated in 2008 and named for two UQ alumni and Australian rugby union representatives, UQ's first Wallaby Eric Francis (King's, 1914–15) and Nigel Kassulke (St Leo's, 1979–81), 2009.

The University of Queensland was hit at once from both sides – a significant reduction in funding and an increase in student numbers. There was one benefit amidst all the changes: from now on the University of Queensland was to be funded on its performance as a university and not just on student numbers. Things would have to change fast though if the

University was to remain competitive. At the time it was ranked thirteen out of nineteen universities in the country in the area of research performance. PhD enrolments were low, due in part to the limited availability of scholarships and other student support. The turnaround was dramatic. By 1990 the University had been awarded nearly $6 million in Australian Research Council funding, placing it in the top four out of thirty universities in the country, a position it has held or bettered ever since. In 1991 the Australian Research Council funding had more than doubled in one year, to just over $13 million. In 1992 a record 24,743 students enrolled at the University, and a general increase in Tertiary Entrance score cut-off points indicated that the academic quality of the 1992 intake was the highest ever to that point. In 1994, 81 per cent of OP1 students – the state's brightest Year 12 students – enrolled at the University. Designated the top performer in gaining financial support for research from industrial sources, the University of Queensland was graduating more PhD students than any other university in Australia.

Postgraduate students now account for 21 per cent of the total student numbers and the Graduate School looks after the interests of those undertaking research higher degrees. The University still has one of the largest PhD enrolments in Australia, and is among the nation's top three universities for PhD completions.

When Vice-Chancellor Wilson arrived at the University, he was immediately impressed by the tremendous potential of work being done on

Many athletes train at UQ. The athletics facilities on Oval No. 5 (the rugby union oval) were chosen by the Italian Olympic Committee for pre-games training for the Sydney Olympics in 2000.

projects such as solar energy in housing and fuel economy in cars; the Julius Kruttschnitt Mineral Research Centre at the University Mine in Indooroopilly was a world leader, while the Department of Agriculture had a multi-million-dollar enterprise in Thailand and was training postgraduates from many other countries in similar activities. There was one obvious weakness. Because the projects were funded externally, the financial, research and intellectual property benefits were leaving the University and not benefiting

Computer Science students talk megabytes with the Duchess of Kent in 1985, during UQ's 75th anniversary celebrations.

the community. This went against one of the founding principles of a 'people's university'. With senate backing, Wilson decided to make it easier for ordinary Queenslanders to seek expert help from the University's departments and faculties. He had been urged by the federal government to look at self-funding measures to upgrade equipment and for research, because over 80 per cent of the budget was being spent on salary costs. Now was the time to act.

In 1982 the University of Queensland Foundation was launched to attract donations from corporations and citizens who recognised the long-term value of research. Largely inspired by Wilson and senate member Sir James Foots, the vision was for a university with financial independence. It was the dawn of a new era for the University of Queensland, one necessary to ensure its survival as the country moved closer to a user-pays system for higher education, although parliamentarians of the past would have been horrified at the thought of the government losing control of the University to the whims of private donors. But the Foundation was part of a larger plan that fitted in with the creation of UniQuest, the University's research and expertise commercialisation company. UniQuest was launched in 1983 by federal Minister for Science and Technology Barry Jones, who conferred the 'blessings of a Labor government on this novel exercise in free enterprise'. UniQuest started with one desk, two chairs and a telephone. From developing, commercialising and managing an extensive intellectual property and asset portfolio, sales of products based on University of Queensland technologies are now running at $5.2 billion a year. Significant benefits of Wilson's vision include UniQuest's 1991 filing of a patent covering the discovery by Professor Ian Frazer and the late Dr Jian Zhou of a

Triple Zed broadcasters, 1980s

Heading home after lectures, on the path beside the Victor and Evelyn Lewis Fountain, presented to the University in 1969

vaccine against the human papilloma virus, known to cause cervical cancer. Commercialisation of this discovery by UniQuest has generated a significant revenue stream for further research, and to date more than 45 million doses of the vaccine have been distributed worldwide. From the Social Sciences, the Triple P Positive Parenting Program commercialising Professor Matt Sanders' research within the School of Psychology has been translated into twenty languages and is currently available to families in seventeen countries. UniQuest is now one of Australia's leading university commercialisation companies and is ranked in the top 10 per cent for university technology transfer internationally.

After six months at the University, Wilson called for a dramatic overhaul of the academic structure. He proposed that the then thirteen faculties and over sixty departments be clustered in five resource groups, each group under the authority of a 'super dean'. These groups (Biological Sciences, Health Sciences, Humanities, Physical Sciences and Engineering, and Social Sciences) would compete against each other for resources. The debate over the changes lasted for two years before the new structure was implemented by the senate and the professorial board in 1983, although the 'super dean' title was replaced by the more appropriate 'pro-vice-chancellor'. Under Wilson, the tutorial system was augmented by postgraduates who were given the opportunity to enhance their full-time research involvement with a modest wage and a teaching apprenticeship.

In 1980 approval was given for a multi-million-dollar extension to the Social Sciences Building, to house Psychology. Money was provided for the planning of a new Clinical Sciences building at Royal Brisbane Hospital and the Staff Club received approval for the linking structures between its two halves. An extension to the Priestley Building to house Computer Science, which had separated from Electrical Engineering in 1969, was approved and a new Veterinary Pathology block was opened. The Alumni Teaching Garden

The refurbished and expanded Biological Sciences Library

The first Great Court race was staged by the UQ
Sports and Physical Recreation Association (now
UQ Sport) as its contribution to the 75th anniversary
celebration in 1985.

for botany was a gift from the Alumni Association, which also contributed over $80,000 in 1982 to build the residential complex at the Goondiwindi Pastoral Veterinary Centre.

Throughout the 1980s people from around the state came to the University campus in greater numbers than ever before. In 1980, 45,000 people attended Expo-Uni at St Lucia, and in 1982 the event attracted over 50,000 visitors. A careers week held in the off year was popular with students and their parents. But students definitely didn't want their parents with them during the Orientation Week festivities. The 'O' Week rampages of the 1980s soon rivalled the fervour of earlier Commemoration celebrations, with pranks, a famous toga party and a pool party at the university swimming complex generating plenty of controversy. Initiation ceremonies at the colleges started making a comeback at around this time, after a crackdown in the 1960s and 1970s had toned them down. Meanwhile, the concept of a 'people's university' had taken hold again as the vice-chancellor attended several graduation ceremonies outside Brisbane, including the first one held outside Australia, in Manila in May 1981. In March 1983 a degree ceremony was held in Boggo Road gaol for inmates who had been enrolled as external students.

In 1985 the University celebrated its seventy-fifth anniversary with a garden party in the Great Court attended by graduates from every decade as far back as 1914. The Duke and Duchess of Kent visited the campus, and at Old Government House the governor's wife, Lady Ramsay, planted a tree propagated from one planted by Lady MacGregor when the University Act was proclaimed by her husband in 1909. The first Great

'O' Week celebrations in the Great Court in 2009, a mix of modern subtropical fashion, entertainment and information gathering

Guests at the launch of *A Place of Light and Learning*, a history of UQ written by Professor Malcolm Thomis as part of the 75th anniversary celebrations, at Old Government House in 1985. Academics no longer wear gowns at such events, with the singular exception of formal graduation ceremonies.

Court Race, modelled on the famous Cambridge race depicted in the Academy-Award-winning film *Chariots of Fire*, drew thousands of spectators who cheered the race winner and runners-up as they received their prizes from the Duchess. The race has been a celebrated annual event ever since.

The practice of conferring honorary degrees on the governor and the premier at significant anniversaries was continued, although Premier Joh Bjelke-Petersen received his at Parliament House weeks later rather than at the campus ceremony. With the famous Fitzgerald Inquiry into corruption which toppled the Queensland state government only a few years away, many staff, students and members of the general public had been opposed

Gatton graduates and friends in high spirits, December 2008. Gatton graduations are held in the Gymnasium on campus. Ipswich graduations are staged at the Ipswich Civic Hall.

The Administration, Matron's and Nurses Quarters of the then Ipswich Hospital for the Insane, later the Challinor Centre, was completed in 1914. When Challinor became the Ipswich campus, a great deal of effort went into the conservation and adaptive reuse of heritage buildings on the site.

These ornate roof ridge vents are an iconic feature of the heritage buildings on the Ipswich campus.

to the premier receiving this honour, and his absence didn't stop protestors turning up and heckling the governor, Sir James Ramsay. The vice-chancellor lamented in his annual report the television coverage given to the small number of noisy protestors 'almost entirely having no connection with the university'.

In 1985, in its second full year of operation, UniQuest made a net profit of nearly $200,000, commercialising the efficient conversion of sugar-cane syrup to ethanol and fructose and the economic conversion of waste products to protein. Meanwhile, the University of Queensland Foundation started allocating funds to university research projects, signifying the start of a golden era for the University in this area. The Queensland Medical Magnetic Resonance Centre opened at the Mater Hospital in Brisbane, a joint project of the University's Department of Radiology, Griffith University's School of Science and the Mater. In 1988 Queensland's first Commonwealth Special Research Centre was established at the University. The Vision, Touch and Hearing Research Centre was set up with government grants of $600,000 a year. The Centre for Molecular Biology and Biotechnology, a forerunner of the Institute for Molecular Bioscience, was also established. In 1989 construction began on the $14.3 million Engineering building, which was the University's largest undertaking since work started on the Forgan Smith Building back in 1937.

The Wilson years also saw the rapid and expensive inclusion of computers in university life. Computer Science was the fastest growing department on campus. In 1985 a $1.2 million mainframe computer was added to the Prentice Computer Centre's network, followed in July 1988 by

The library at the Ipswich campus, 2003, looks more like a subtropical garden than a traditional library. It provides a tranquil place for study.

Animal studies students at Gatton, May 2008

a million-dollar, state-of-the-art computer system to provide online access to the university library catalogue. The Unisys computer system handled more than 20,000 transactions daily and would eventually replace the card catalogue. In August 1990 the supercomputer *Charlotte* was installed at the Centre for Information Technology Research following a $1.3 million Australian Research Council grant, and five years later a $3 million silicon graphics supercomputer, believed to be the most powerful parallel computing system in Australia, was installed on campus.

During the 1980s some of the more traditional faculties celebrated their fiftieth anniversaries: Law and Dentistry in 1985 and Medicine the following year. A new small-animals hospital opened at the St Lucia campus as part of the Veterinary Science School's fiftieth anniversary celebrations. In other significant milestones, the university senate resolved to establish a senate standing committee on the status of women to promote equal opportunities in study and employment at the University. Not long afterwards, the University's first equal opportunity coordinator was appointed. The Alumni Book Fair held over several days in Mayne Hall became a biennial event, helping to raise money for university purposes, and in 1988 the University awarded its 75,000th degree, to a Bachelor of Medical Science graduate.

Rallies and demonstrations came back to campus in 1981. Students and over 100 staff, who gave up a day's pay, protested on 20 May against a government proposal to introduce loans and fees for second and higher

degrees. Students occupied the top floor of the JD Story
Administration Building to stop the senate from administering the
charges, even though the senate was not in favour of them either.
More demonstrations were held in 1982, including an all-night
'study-in' at the Law Library in April to highlight the funding plight
of the Faculty of Law, which received national attention. The
voices of the law undergraduates were heard but the funding
wheels turned slowly. They would have to wait until October
1990 when the Queensland governor Sir Walter Campbell, a
Law alumnus and former chancellor, opened the $3.25 million
redevelopment of the TC Beirne School of Law, the design of
which won a Royal Australian Institute of Architects award for a
non-residential design. In May 1982 students invaded a senate
meeting as part of their campaign to extend the opening hours of
the library. On 28 July there was another top-floor demonstration
after a Great Court rally against federal government higher-
education policies. The rally was organised by the Staff
Association and the Student Union.

It has often been said that Brisbane came of age during
World Expo 88, and the University of Queensland certainly took
full advantage of the international attention, with the UNIvations
pavilion, partly sponsored by the University, attracting over a
million people. The land, sea and space communications displays
were showcased under the model of a scram jet engine being
developed in the Mechanical Engineering Department. In 1989
the largest capital works program at St Lucia since the early 1970s got under
way with construction of buildings worth up to $60 million.

Framed by the elegant sandstone columns, this is just
one of the many cafés on the St Lucia campus.

Public transport is the 'green' option for many students and staff. At peak hour the St Lucia campus is the second-top destination in Brisbane after the CBD.

The 1990s signalled another change of direction for the University. The pace of technological change meant that the University needed to embrace new directions underpinned by new technologies.

In 1999 the interactive, high-technology campus at Ipswich, about 40 kilometres west of Brisbane, came into operation, where students could study using state-of-the art, web-enabled learning and teaching methods. The campus is the site of the former Challinor Centre, which was used as a treatment place for people with mental illness, dating back to 1878. At Ipswich, programs are currently available in Business, Education, Health Sciences, Human Services, Midwifery and Nursing. In 2009 students undertook Medicine at Ipswich for the first time, and the campus is now assuming a focus on education for the health industries.

In February 1990 Chancellor Sir James Foots opened the $1.8 million extension to the University of Queensland Staff and Graduates Club, and in June 1990 MIM Holdings Ltd chairman Sir Bruce Watson opened the $16 million Hawken Engineering Building, the nerve centre for the five engineering departments and the University's largest single building outside the Great Court. The building features the 396-seat Raybould Lecture Theatre, named after graduate and benefactor Miss Ethel Raybould, Queensland's first female university mathematics lecturer.

Because of the massive expansion of the campus, when staff and student numbers were increasing at the same time as the existing car parks were being encroached on by new buildings, the dreaded issue of paid parking raised its head (it had been mentioned several times in previous annual reports). In October 1990 the university senate resolved to introduce paid parking at the St Lucia, Herston and Turbot Street sites from 1991. A three-tier permit system, supplemented by parking meters and pay-and-display machines in designated areas, condemned a new generation of university students to the dangers of parking inspectors. Those who ran the gauntlet of free parking when running late for lectures usually found their cars with a ticket under the wiper blades.

Meeting with friends on the St Lucia campus

Dr Tara Walker and Dr Tom Keeble at the Queensland Brain Institute are seeking to discover factors that stimulate neural stem cells for the treatment of ageing dementia.

In March 1991 the University secured its largest ever private research contract, valued at $55 million, under a government-approved syndicated research and development scheme, and in June 1991 the federal Minister for Science and Technology, Simon Crean, commissioned a $1.5 million electron microscope, purchased jointly with Queensland Railways, Griffith University, Queensland University of Technology and the Australian Research Council. In 1993 the University hosted the inaugural Australian University Games, with more than 5,000 competitors from Australia and overseas. The host university's 400-strong team won by more than 100 points and the games contributed an estimated $4 million to the local economy.

A major appeal in 1994 enabled the University to restore Brisbane's Customs House as an educational and cultural resource for the state, an achievement that Professor Wilson listed as one of his proudest. The following year the Australian government selected the University and the Walter and Eliza Hall Institute of Medical Research as the location for the world's first-known multi-purpose genetic research site – the $10 million Australian Genome Research Facility.

By the middle of the hectic 1990s, the protest years of the 1960s and 1970s and the rebellious excesses of the 1980s were a distant memory. The University was run like a business. In his annual reports Wilson likened the institution to a public company beholden to its shareholders – the taxpayers of Australia, the students, the academic staff and the alumni. The arrival of the fledgling Internet meant that there was no time to

The General Purpose South Building, which awaits a permanent name, has an elegant setting overlooking one of the lakes at St Lucia campus.

Every year the Aboriginal and Torres Strait Islander Studies Unit organises an orientation camp for new Indigenous students. Information sessions on the UQ libraries are included in the orientation activities.

rest if the University wanted to remain competitive in the information age. Things were only going to get faster.

In 1996 the former vice-chancellor of Victoria's Deakin University, Professor John Hay, was given the task of taking the University of Queensland into the new millennium. Professor Hay, a gifted orator and scholar with degrees in literature from the University of Western Australia and Cambridge, would oversee a new era of growth and success across a diversity of fields.

The Forgan Smith Building, the grand entry to the Great Court, with blue lighting for World Diabetes Day 2008

CHAPTER 5

BEYOND 2000

The UQ Art Museum in the James and Mary Emelia Mayne Centre holds a large permanent collection and also hosts regular temporary exhibitions. *Reincarnation – Mao, Buddha & I* by Liu Xiao Xian was part of a 2008 exhibition.

NO ONE KNEW IT at the time, but a meeting at Brisbane's Irish Club on St Patrick's Day in 1998 signified a major turning point in the history of the University of Queensland. Over lunch, newly installed vice-chancellor John Hay and Irish-American billionaire businessman Charles 'Chuck' Feeney from The Atlantic Philanthropies established a relationship that would result in a spectacular series of capital works programs at St Lucia. The result was world-class research institutes and a modern art gallery that have made the University of Queensland the envy of universities around the world while enriching Brisbane and the nation. The research institutes also brought to a halt the 'brain drain' that had been so damaging to Queensland in the past. They are able to attract and retain the best students and researchers in Australia, and indeed the world, while also holding onto precious local talent. Australia's brightest research students no longer have to travel overseas to get the research experience and opportunities they crave.

Prior to and not long after the historic Irish Club meeting, the University still had much to celebrate, including its first Nobel laureate: graduate Professor Peter Doherty. An honorary professor in the Department of Pathology, he received the 1996 Nobel Prize for medicine jointly with Professor Rolf Zinkernagel of Switzerland for discovering how the immune system recognises virus-infected cells. The following year the University was one of three in Australia to become foundation members of Universitas 21, an elite international consortium limited to twenty-one members. In 1998 *The Good Universities Guide* awarded it the coveted title of University of the Year, and in the following year the University was placed second nationally in the Commonwealth-funded Research Quantum based on overall research performance.

Much like his predecessor, Professor Hay's first year as vice-chancellor featured massive changes in higher education throughout Australia. In 1996 a new Howard Coalition government adjusted the university fee structure, which saw HECS charges rise by an average of 40 per cent. Fees were now to be paid on the perceived value of the university courses. Students studying Law and Medicine would in theory be earning the most when they graduated and so they would be charged HECS at the highest rate. Arts students, who wouldn't be earning as much, were in the lowest band. Universities were also given the option to create full-fee places for students

The Antiquities Museum in the Michie Building has strong support from former staff, students and benefactors. It regularly plays host to secondary students studying ancient history, giving them a real sense of modern archaeology and a first-hand experience of artefacts.

Carving of a ringtail possum, another explicitly Australian element in the Great Court

Chemical engineer Dr John Zhu, who is advancing important research into clean energy and greenhouse gas reduction to secure the future health of our planet

who didn't qualify for a HECS place. If students could afford to pay in full the expensive up-front fees, there was a limited number of places that were offered on a merit basis at cut-offs marginally below those required for Commonwealth-supported places.

In preparation for the changing landscape, Hay decided to dramatically overhaul the academic structure at the University for the 1997 academic year. The senate approved a new seven-faculty academic structure, championed by Hay as being a 'flatter, leaner system', designed to streamline and integrate decision-making and resource management. Its flexibility would be tested again in 2005 when the federal government deregulated university fees.

The next twelve years under Hay would see a whirlwind of activity. The building projects would not just provide places in which to conduct research and learning but would also improve the beauty and feel of the campus. It was no secret that Hay was mortified by some of the so-called 'cheap and nasty' buildings that had been erected at St Lucia after the war without regard for their integrity among the more traditional architecture. Determined to improve the aesthetics of the campus, he collaborated with Alasdair McClintock, UQ Property and Facilities director, to make a plan. The University's efforts to create a high-quality built environment at all its campuses and research sites would earn it the 2008 Australian Institute of Architects (AIA Queensland) President's Prize.

In December of Hay's first year, plans were announced to develop an Institute for Molecular Bioscience (IMB) at St Lucia, where scientists could work to decipher the information contained in the genes, molecules and proteins of humans, plants and animals. This would be the first in a series of institutes brought to the University in partnership with The Atlantic Philanthropies, the state government's 'Smart State' initiative, and the Commonwealth government. The state started things off with a $77.5 million pledge over ten years to make the IMB a reality, while also offering a further $10 million over three years for supercomputing. The $105 million Queensland Bioscience Precinct at St Lucia housing the IMB and several CSIRO divisions opened in 2003. The new institute will spawn new drugs and treatments and generate new industries.

In 2002 a $33 million research complex opened at Princess Alexandra Hospital (PAH) as the new home for a University of Queensland research group pioneering vaccines against cervical cancer and genital warts. Professor Ian Frazer was named head of the Centre for Immunology and Cancer Research, later to be incorporated into the UQ Diamantina Institute for Cancer, Immunology and Metabolic Medicine. In September 2002 the $20 million multi-purpose UQ Centre was opened at St Lucia to provide a modern venue for a variety of events, including the graduation ceremonies.

In 2004 the James and Mary Emelia Mayne Centre opened at St Lucia, transforming the old Mayne Hall into an art museum, which features thousands of works by international and Australian artists and is Queensland's second largest public art collection. A national collection of artists' self-portraits is the first of its kind in the country, and a variety of exhibitions attracts many visitors to the campus each year. Not everyone was celebrating the creation of the Art Museum, however, as it meant the loss of a music performance venue that had been enjoyed by the public.

Modern technology is a part of every student's life, with wi-fi networks facilitating outdoor study sessions.

The Australian Institute of Bioengineering and Nanotechnology (AIBN), combining the skills of engineers, chemists, biologists and computational scientists, was opened by the premier Peter Beattie at St Lucia in October 2006, while the state government also pledged $10 million and the University about $20 million to help build the Sustainable Minerals Institute at St Lucia.

In 2006 the state government promised $100 million for a Translational Research Institute (TRI) to be built at the Princess Alexandra Hospital, a

Open Day at Gatton, August 2009

sum that was matched a year later by the Commonwealth government. The TRI is a partnership between the University of Queensland, the Queensland University of Technology (QUT), Princess Alexandra Hospital, Mater Medical Research Institute (MMRI) and the state government, designed to translate laboratory success into benefits for patients, filling a crucial gap in Australia's medical research capacity. This collaborative partnership was key in attracting a $50 million Founding Chairman's grant from The Atlantic Philanthropies, the single largest gift to one medical or higher education institution in the nation's history. The facility will house the University of Queensland's Diamantina Institute for Cancer, Immunology and Metabolic Medicine, along with other centres.

The Hay years finished with the opening of the $63 million Queensland Brain Institute at St Lucia and the $66 million Centre for Clinical Research beside the Royal Brisbane and Women's Hospital in Herston, and he oversaw the development and early construction of stage one of the $33 million Centre for Advanced Animal Science at the Gatton campus. The Institute for Social Science Research (ISSR) was established in 2007 to enhance social science research at the University and to contribute nationally to the development of social sciences in Australia. The ISSR has an annual budget of $11 million and employs around 100 people.

The results of all the research-intensive expenditure are already starting to filter through. In January 2009 there was a major research breakthrough in the fight against dengue fever, which infects millions of

Residents of International House, who come to UQ from across the world, prepare for Soirée, a multicultural festival that has been staged annually since 1967.

people around the world each year and kills around 20,000. Following a $10 million grant from the Bill and Melinda Gates Foundation, a research team at the University of Queensland led by Professor Scott O'Neill was able to halve the lifespan of female mosquitoes that carry the tropical disease. In August 2009 Professor John Zhu from the university's School of Chemical Engineering successfully tested technology that delivers twice the normal power from coal while reducing harmful greenhouse emissions. From Hubei province in central China, Dr Zhu worked in a steel factory in China while studying engineering and he dreamed of creating a cleaner environment. The world-first breakthrough could provide a billion-dollar windfall for the state and the University while revolutionising the way the world uses coal.

Meanwhile, a number of University researchers have been awarded International Science Linkages Grants, which support collaboration with international partners on cutting-edge science and technology. In the coming years University scientists will travel to research institutions in China, Japan, Korea, Taiwan, Europe and North America to work on a variety of projects, from the treatment of burns victims to improvements in agriculture. For example, in 2010 Professor Chen Chen from the School of Biomedical Sciences will investigate new treatments for diabetes-related heart disease. Professor Chen will work in collaboration with Professor Wei-jin Zang at China's Xi'an Jiaotong University.

Perhaps one of the finest moments of the 'noughties', as the first decade of the new century was referred to in the media, came in late 2006 with the opening of the 'Green Bridge', later named the Eleanor Schonell

Professor Ian Frazer, the 2006 Australian of the Year. As Director of the UQ Diamantina Institute for Cancer, Immunology and Metabolic Medicine, he is one of the most recognised faces of UQ nationally and internationally.

The centenary of the Foundation Building on the Gatton campus was marked in 1997.

Bridge. Australia's first pedestrian, cycle and bus bridge has brought the St Lucia campus within a ten-minute bus ride of South Bank and the CBD and opened up access to the south-eastern suburbs. The bridge has also forged close links between the Princess Alexandra Hospital precinct and the University and its research activity and infrastructure. The Pharmacy Australia Centre of Excellence (PACE) under construction in the Princess Alexandra Hospital precinct is a visionary concept jointly developed by the

The Architecture and Music Library, one of UQ's
fourteen libraries

University and the pharmacy profession in 2000 that will create a leading facility for pharmaceutical research, education and commercialisation. The School of Pharmacy relocated to the high-tech facilities at PACE at the beginning of the 2010 academic year, allowing the school to significantly increase its undergraduate and postgraduate student body, and its research capacity.

The Australian Institute of Bioengineering and
Nanotechnology Building, the interior of which is
designed to encourage multidisciplinary interaction

Professor Scott O'Neill leads dengue fever research funded by the Bill and Melinda Gates Foundation. Roxanna Lane assisted with this project for a time.

From the mid-2000s there was a strong focus on the Gatton campus, which has been transformed into Australia's best precinct for animal-related research and teaching. Construction started in February 2007 on the Centre for Advanced Animal Science and the next year on the new and refurbished School of Veterinary Science facilities. A new rural clinical school teaching and learning centre opened at Toowoomba, highlighting investment in the clinical schools model. As the decade draws to a close, the University of Queensland is still ranked among Australia's top universities for research funding, increasing its research income by more than 60 per cent since 2003.

In 1988, under Brian Wilson, the University was the first Australian university to introduce teaching awards. Today, excellence in teaching and learning is encouraged through a variety of teaching awards and special grants, as well as specialist support for skills enhancement offered by the Teaching and Educational Development Institute and the Centre for Educational Innovation and Technology. For over ten years the University has been the most successful Australian university in winning awards for teaching excellence and for programs that enhance learning. In 2007, a new category of academic staff, teaching-focused academics, was created to allow academics to pursue scholarship in teaching within their academic discipline.

The University places great emphasis on improving the student experience. Modern student learning spaces have replaced old lecture theatres and seminar rooms. E-learning initiatives bring the latest technology into the learning process. Undergraduate students have improved access to research experience and they can enjoy the benefits of a range of internship and overseas study opportunities.

The University of Queensland's $54 million 'General Purpose North 4' building, at the junction of Campbell Road and University Drive, was officially opened in July 2008 and was later renamed the Sir Llew Edwards Building, after the much-admired twelfth chancellor, who was a medical student at the University in the 1960s. The building, one of the most impressive new structures at St Lucia, incorporates two of Sir Llew's great passions – international education, and teaching and learning. Funded by the federal government, the building's $2.5 million Advanced Concepts Teaching Space (ACTS) features futuristic technology not expected to be commonplace in other universities for at least a decade. Set across three levels, the ACTS hosts systems that allow students to download lectures on to their iPods, laptops or mobile phones. On the flipside, students can use advanced projection systems to screen their work to the whole class, while individual touch-screens enable instantaneous polling and voting on topics under discussion. Lecturers can get immediate feedback from students on how well key concepts are being understood. To maximise student participation, questions can be typed in rather than asked out loud, a feature that helps overcome student shyness. The screens give students the option to move through slides at their own pace or even to branch off into additional material. A translation system is currently being developed to allow students whose first language is not English to instantly look up unfamiliar terms.

Rhyl Hinwood's striking mural, *The Art of Agriculture*, on the Gatton campus

The John Hay Building, Queensland Biosciences
Precinct, which was built on the site of the CSIRO
Cunningham Laboratories, 2007

At just over 1,400 hectares, the enormous size of the St Lucia campus can be rather daunting to new students, but the University has comprehensive student advice services to help them navigate their way around. The choice of 370 degrees and 5,600 subjects can also be overwhelming, but at carefully designed information evenings across all campuses students have the chance to chat to staff about study options and alternative pathways into preferred programs. At these sessions, representatives from faculties, Admissions, Scholarships and Student Recruitment are on hand to answer questions about entry requirements, prerequisites and the QTAC process. The academic needs of postgraduate students are also catered for with programs for thesis writing, literature review and understanding research policies. When the University of Queensland took in its first students in 1911, a young woman, Hilda Brotherton, travelled from Rockhampton to Brisbane to begin her biology degree at the Old Government House site. She wrote home that she had no idea how to construct a first-year course and that the staff she asked for help seemed just as confused as she was. Student support services have come a long way from those early days.

Vice-Chancellor John Hay, philanthropist Chuck Feeney and former premier and UQ alumnus Peter Beattie at the official opening of the Queensland Brain Institute in November 2007

With just under 9,000 international students among the 40,000 studying at the various campuses, the University has worked hard to make their experience as 'easy and enjoyable' as possible. Student Services offers workshops for these students, with the opportunity for them to liaise with an international student advisor, who can provide information about campus facilities, enrolment, public transport and even on-campus banking. Students also receive assistance with their university social life. Programs tailored specifically for international students include the Mates@UQ program, which

The Emmanuel College Pipe Band shows what it can do, at 'O' Week, 2009.

UQ regularly holds graduation ceremonies overseas.
This ceremony, presided over by Chancellor Sir Llew
Edwards, Vice-Chancellor John Hay and other senior
UQ staff, took place in Kuala Lumpur in 2004.

Chancellor John Story, UQ's thirteenth chancellor, congratulates a graduate, Li Feifei (Master of Journalism), in 2009.

encourages a social and academic network between Australian students and international students. There is no better example of the successful integration of international students into campus life than that of Randal Pittelli from the United States, who studied for a Bachelor of Medicine and Bachelor of Surgery (MBBS) while also president for a time of the UQ Medical Society. With membership of around 800 students, the Medical Society runs social events and has representatives on academic committees that influence Medical School policy. Randal says he chose the University's medical program over others around the world because he was looking for a cultural difference set among a great learning environment. 'Brisbane has all the amenities of a large city yet still has that big town feel, where people are curious and approachable, and the city isn't too large to escape whenever you want. Queensland's nearly idyllic weather was an additional draw.' Randal found the opportunity that the Medical School offers for clinical placements overseas and in rural areas appealing. It was also the only school offering first-year electives, during one of which he went to the Solomon Islands for seven weeks.

China, Malaysia and Singapore are the University's top three source countries for international students. When Chinese student Jun Xiong (Sara), who studied for a Bachelor of Engineering (Mechanical) degree, decided she wanted to complete her university degree overseas, her first priorities, she says, were safety and a quality education. She decided to study at the University of Queensland because its mechanical engineering program was one of the best in Australia. 'Mechanical engineering is a booming industry at the moment, so by the time I graduate there will be a high demand for people with my qualifications,' she wrote on the UQ website, which contains the stories of many students from around the world and locally. 'I think people here have a very positive attitude to life – they really enjoy their lives and that's another reason why I like it here. I feel at home and have made lots of friends from different countries.'

A typical day in the life of a current student involves juggling commitments to class contact, to study time in the library or at home (mainly accessing electronic sources), and to their part-time jobs, which increasing numbers of students are finding necessary. In contrast to earlier generations of students, some are back and forth to campus multiple times on the one day and many are accessing library holdings throughout the night.

Of the thousands of staff at the University, the great majority of academics still have their own offices, some in historic buildings like Forgan Smith, others in St Lucia's brand new research institutes. The majority of administration staff and library staff are in open-plan offices. Many of the support staff are long-serving, with up to thirty each year invited to a special function to recognise their twenty-five years of service. Typical teaching and research

The St Lucia campus Indoor Sports Pavilion has been host to a variety of sports.

The early academics wouldn't recognise today's modern teaching spaces, where chalk has almost entirely given way to a high-tech learning environment.

staff members are expected to teach and coordinate various courses, supervise research and honours students, hold a number of research grants and produce publications, participate in the marking of assessment items and perform service roles within their school or for the University. It's possible that they spend even more time on the Internet than their students do, with at least an hour or more a day responding to emails. Even PhD theses are now submitted digitally rather than in bound volumes, overturning hundreds of years of academic tradition.

Since its inception one hundred years ago, the senate has had an uncanny knack of selecting strong, capable leaders driven by a passion for education (the number one requirement) while also possessing character traits suited to handling the difficult and complex issues of their day. JD Story was an excellent administrator and organiser who used his connections within the state government to great advantage. Professor Fred Schonell embraced the new medium of television and with it public relations and advertising, fostering relationships with business and, most importantly, opening the lines of communication between the administration and the students at a time when the students needed a voice. Sir Zelman Cowen's civil liberties background and considerable diplomatic skills kept potential disaster at bay as political and social turmoil tore through the campus, although never tearing it apart. Professor Brian Wilson's vision, research drive and entrepreneurial flair steered the University through financially turbulent times as federal government funding stumbled and the system moved closer towards the user-pays model we know today. Professor John Hay's extraordinary fundraising ability enabled the university to take full advantage of the technological breakthroughs in interactive learning and research, while his love of architecture transformed the campus and created spaces of exceptional beauty. In Vice-Chancellor Professor Paul Greenfield, who took over in 2008, the University and the state have found a champion of the environment and sustainability. Not long after he took over, the senate endorsed the establishment of the University's seventh institute, the Global Change Institute.

Professor Greenfield began his academic career at the University of Queensland in 1975 as a lecturer in Chemical Engineering, and by 2004 he had been named one of Australia's one hundred most influential engineers. His academic interest in sustainability has seen him chairing the South East Queensland

With dedicated cycling tracks and a purpose-built bridge, pedal power has become a popular alternative to buses and cars.

The modern bus shelter at the University Lakes bus stop at the St Lucia end of the Eleanor Schonell Bridge

Healthy Waterways Partnership, which over the past ten years has become the national benchmark for waterways management. Already he has stamped his mark on the University's future direction, vowing to continue with the bioscience and higher-education success of the past while enhancing the University's already considerable standing in the international community. 'Learning', 'discovery' and 'engagement' are key words in the University's mission statement.

As the University of Queensland celebrates its centenary, it is currently placed among the top fifty universities in the World University Rankings, it has won more national teaching awards and boasts a graduate employment rate 5 per cent higher than any other Australian university. Bachelor degree graduates in their first full-time employment reported median starting salaries of $50,000 for males and $47,000 for females. Of those in their first full-time employment, the higher-end salaries included dentistry, software engineering, environmental science, research and business analysis, physiotherapy, mining engineering, chemical and mechanical engineering, investment banking and medicine. The three most popular programs by enrolment are Bachelor of Arts, Doctor of Philosophy and Bachelor of Engineering. From three faculties in 1911, the University now has seven: Arts; Business, Economics and Law (BEL); Engineering, Architecture and Information Technology (EAIT); Health Sciences; Natural Resources, Agriculture and Veterinary Science (NRAVS); Science; and Social and Behavioural Sciences (SBS).

From humble and uncertain beginnings a century ago, the University of Queensland now stands proudly as a world leader in collaborative learning, teaching and research. And regardless of the changes and challenges that lie ahead, one founding principle is sure to endure: the University of Queensland will remain the people's university.

Vice-Chancellor Professor Paul Greenfield with first-year students, 'O' Week, 2008

ACKNOWLEDGMENTS

WRITING A CENTENARY HISTORY for a prestigious institution such as the University of Queensland was a daunting but enjoyable challenge. In terms of research, a debt of gratitude is owed to Professor Malcolm Thomis whose excellent book *A Place of Light and Learning* was an invaluable guide while navigating UQ's first seventy-five years. The University's annual reports were a rich source of information for the last twenty-five years.

Thanks also to the staff at the State Library and the University's Fryer Library, and to the *Courier-Mail* and the *Sunday Mail* for use of their information services, made easier for the later chapters of the book thanks to the wonders of the Internet and Newstext. During my cadetship at Queensland Newspapers in Bowen Hills and afterwards as a graded journalist, there were frequent trips to the St Lucia campus accompanied by a photographer to do picture stories. Nearly twenty years on and UQ is even more media savvy with a website full of news stories through its re-named Office of Marketing and Communications, whose help was enormous in highlighting the work of the various research institutes and faculties.

Thanks to Ellen Juhasz of the UQ Centenary Secretariat for her tireless work in answering questions and for her support in general, to university archivist Bruce Ibsen, to Professor Peter Spearritt whose advice resulted in a more thorough history, and to all those who read drafts and helped with images, including Maryse Scott, Marg Lavery, Fiona Kennedy, Wilber Williams, Don Munro, Spencer Routh, Shannon Price, the Senior Deputy Vice-Chancellor Michael Keniger and Vice-Chancellor Paul Greenfield. Thanks to Madonna Duffy, Publisher at the University of Queensland Press, who performed minor miracles getting this project together, and to editor Felicity McKenzie for her guidance.

Over the past one hundred years there have been many people who have contributed to UQ's success through their hard work, passion and initiative. The fact that it has not been possible to mention them all in the narrative in no way diminishes the enormity of their achievements.

Photo credits
The images used in this book have been kindly provided and used courtesy of the UQ Office of Marketing and Communication, the Fryer Library, UQ Archives and the UQ Museum of IT, and QUT Marketing and Communication (p. 3), the Kruger family (p. 28), St Leo's College (p. 32), Cromwell College (p. 32), Grace College (p. 36), the State Library of Queensland (p. 62), Women's College (p. 83), King's College (p. 84) and International House (p. 111).

INDEX